Conversational
SPANISH
in 7 Days

*Master Language Survival Skills
in Just One Week!*

Shirley Baldwin and Sarah Boas

New York   Chicago   San Francisco   Lisbon   London   Madrid   Mexico City
Milan   New Delhi   San Juan   Seoul   Singapore   Sydney   Toronto

The McGraw·Hill Companies

Originally published by Hodder & Stoughton Publishers.

Copyright © 1988 by Shirley Baldwin and Sarah Boas and © 2004 by The McGraw-Hill Companies, Inc. All rights reserved. Printed in Hong Kong. Except as permitted under the United States Copyright Act of 1976, no part of this publication may be reproduced or distributed in any form or by any means, or stored in a database or retrieval system, without the prior written permission of the publisher.

12 13 14 15 16 17 18 19   WKT/WKT   14 13

ISBN 978-0-07-143232-0 (package)
MHID   0-07-143232-9 (package)

ISBN 978-0-07-143236-8 (book)
MHID   0-07-143236-1 (book)

Library of Congress Cataloging-in-Publication Data

Baldwin, Shirley.
       Conversational Spanish in 7 days / Shirley Baldwin and Sarah Boas.
              p.   cm.
       ISBN 0-07-143236-1 (book) — ISBN 0-07-143232-9 (package)
       1. Spanish language—Conversation and phrase books—English.   I. Title:
Conversational Spanish in seven days.   II. Boas, Sarah.   III. Title

       PC4121.B23   2004
       468.3'421—dc22   2004052746

Acknowledgments

The authors and publishers are grateful to the following for supplying photographs or illustrations:
Barnaby's Picture Library (pp. 9, 21, 30, 59)
J. Allan Cash Ltd. (pp. 1, 6, 7, 12, 16, 18, 19, 23, 24, 26, 34, 38, 40, 47, 50, 53, 57, 62, 67, 71)
D. J. Fox (pp. 30, 42, 55)

McGraw-Hill books are available at special quantity discounts to use as premiums and sales promotions or for use in corporate training programs. To contact a representative, please e-mail us at bulksales@mcgraw-hill.com.

This book is printed on acid-free paper.

CONTENTS

Conversational Spanish in 7 Days is a short course that will equip you to deal with everyday situations when you visit a Spanish-speaking country.

The course is divided into 7 units, each corresponding to a day in the life of Carmen (a journalist), her husband, Tom, and their two teenage children during their week in Spain. Each unit begins with a dialogue, which introduces the essential vocabulary in context. The phrasebook section lists these and other useful phrases and defines them in English. Within the units there are also sections giving basic grammatical explanations and a number of practice activities designed to be useful as well as fun. Answers can be checked in the back of the book. Also available with this book are 2 CDs to help you practice your Spanish.

A note about the currency used in this book. In 2002, 12 countries in the European Union, including Spain, adopted the Euro as the national currency. In this book, the dialogues and text refer to the former currency of Spain, the *peseta*, which is abbreviated as *pta* in some of the text and the photos.

Pronunciation

1 Pronounce each part of every word; Spanish sounds very much as it is written.
2 Emphasize the second-to-last syllable of every word which ends with a vowel or **n** or **s**.
3 Emphasize the last syllable of every word which ends in a consonant other than **n** or **s**. (Exceptions to these rules carry a written accent.)

Vowels: do not vary their sounds as in English:

a as *a* in *father*; la, mamá
e as in *next*; este, señor
i as *ee* in *meek*; mi, marido
  Before another vowel:
  like **y**; día [deeya], bien
o as in *go*; coche, como

u as *oo* in *moose*; lunes, mucho
  Before another vowel or **y**:
  like **w**; bueno [bwehno], muy [mwee]
  After **q** and in **gue/gui**:
  u is silent; aquí [akee], seguida

Consonants: similar to English but with the following exceptions:

b Between vowels:
  almost **v**; bebida, trabajo
c Before **a, o, u**:
  like *kilo*; como, coche
  Before **e, i**:
  like *thanks*; gracias, hace
ch like *chair*; mucho, chico
d Between vowels & at end of words:
  almost like *th*; seguida, verdad
g Before **a, o, u**: like *gap*; gusto
  Before **e, i**: like *henna*; general

h always silent; hija, hotel
j like *ham*; hija, ajo
ll like *yolk*; llamo [yahmo]
ñ like *onion*; señor, señora
qu like *kilo*; que, aquí
r always sounded, sometimes rolled: verdad
rr strongly rolled: correos, corrida
s like *sun*; sí, soy
v mixture of **b** and **v**; vamos
z like *thank*; plaza, zapato

SAYING HELLO

Arrival   When arriving in Spain, you will find customs (**Aduana**) and passport procedures standard and easy to follow, because most information is given in English as well as Spanish.

mucho gusto/pleased to meet you

Carmen Roberts, a Spanish journalist working in London, has been sent to Madrid to research a story. She is with her husband, Tom, and their two children, Luisa and Miguel. The family is met in Madrid by Andrés Valbuena, a fellow journalist.

Andrés: **Hola. Buenos días. ¿Es usted la señora Roberts, por favor?**

Carmen: **Sí, soy** Carmen Roberts. **¿Cómo se llama usted?**

Andrés: **Me llamo** Andrés Valbuena. **Encantado,** señora Roberts.

Carmen: **Encantada.** Le presento a mi marido, Tom.

Andrés: **Mucho gusto, señor.**

Carmen: **Y esta es mi hija,** Luisa, y este (sees Miguel looking at some magazines) es mi hijo. ¡Miguel, venga! Vamos en coche con el señor Valbuena.

1

On the way to the office, Luisa and Miguel are dropped off at their aunt's apartment. Luisa is greeted by Juan, her 19-year-old Spanish cousin.

Juan: **¡Hola! ¿Qué tal**, Luisa?
Luisa: **Muy bien, ¿y tú, cómo estás?**
Juan: Pues, **bien, gracias**. ¡Hola, Miguel! ¿Qué tal?
Miguel: Bien, gracias.
Juan: Dame tus maletas. (He picks up the suitcases)
Luisa: **Gracias**, primo, eres muy amable.
Juan: **De nada**.
Luisa: Y tu madre, ¿cómo está?
Juan: Mi madre está bien. (Calls) ¡Mamá! Aquí están Luisa y Miguel.
Pilar: ¡Hola! ¡Qué bien, Luisa y Miguel!

Saying hello

Hola. Buenos días.	Hello. Good morning.
Buenas tardes.	Good afternoon./Good evening.
Buenas noches.	Good evening./Good night.

Addressing people in Spanish In Spanish you address a man as **señor** (Mr.), a woman as **señora** (Mrs.), and a girl or young unmarried woman as **señorita** (Miss). It is normal to shake hands both when meeting someone for the first time and also when saying *Hello* or *Goodbye* to a friend or acquaintance. Note that there is a formal and informal way of saying "you." Use the formal **usted** form (the third person of the verb) until you know somebody well, then change to the **tú** form (the second person). In the family and among friends and younger people, the informal form is very frequently used.

Meeting people

¿Cómo se llama usted?	What's your name? (formal)
¿Cómo te llamas?	What's your name? (informal)
Me llamo . . ./Soy . . .	My name is . . ./I am . . .
¿Cómo se llama?	What's his/her name?
Se llama . . .	His/her name is . . .
¿Es usted la señora Valbuena?	Are you Mrs. Valbuena?
Este es . . . (mi hijo)	This is . . . (my son)
Esta es . . . (mi hija)	This is . . . (my daughter)
Le presento a . . .	May I introduce you to . . . (formal)
. . . mi esposa, mi marido	. . . my wife, my husband
. . . mi amigo, mi amiga	. . . my friend
Te presento a . . .	Let me introduce you to . . . (informal)
Encantado./Encantada.	Pleased to meet you. (said by a man/a woman)
Mucho gusto./Tanto gusto.	Pleased to meet you.

Asking how someone is

¿Cómo está usted?	How are you? (formal)
Muy bien, gracias, ¿y usted?	Very well, thank you, and you?
¿Cómo estás?	How are you? (informal)
¿Qué tal? ¿Qué hay?	How are things? How's it going?
Muy bien, ¿y tú?	Fine (thanks), and you?
Bien.	O.K.
¿Cómo está?	How is he/she?
Está bien.	He/she is well.

Yes and No

Sí/No   Yes/No

Saying please and thank you

Por favor/Gracias	Please/Thank you
Muchas gracias.	Thank you very much.
Eres muy amable.	You are very kind. (informal)
De nada./No hay de qué.	You're welcome./Don't mention it.

OTHER USEFUL PHRASES

¡Venga!	Come here!
Vamos en coche	We are going by car
con el señor Valbuena	with Mr. Valbuena
Dame tu maleta.	Give me your suitcase.
Tu madre/Mi madre	Your mother/My mother
¡Qué bien!	How nice!

the way it works

People and things

In Spanish words for both people and things are said to be either masculine or feminine. The word for "the" is:

el for a masculine word: **el** señor (man), **el** coche (car);

la for a feminine word: **la** señora (lady), **la** maleta (suitcase).

Most words ending in -o are masculine (**el** hij**o** = son, **el** marid**o** = husband) and most words ending in -a are feminine (**la** espos**a** = wife, **la** malet**a** = suitcase). But there are several other endings and it is a good idea to learn each word together with **el** or **la**, e.g., el coche = car (-e is usually masculine). Don't worry if you get it wrong. You'll usually be understood!

To make a word plural

El becomes **los**, and la becomes **las**. The ending of the word changes: add **-s** to words ending in a vowel and **-es** to words ending in a consonant: e.g., **las** malet**as** (the suitcases), **los** señor**es** (the men).

Who are you?/What are you?

Soy Carmen Roberts.   I am Carmen Roberts.
Eres muy amable.   You are very kind.
¿Es usted el señor Valbuena?   Are you Mr. Valbuena?

You will see that there are two verbs in Spanish meaning "to be." The one we'll learn first is **ser**. Here is the pattern of its present tense:

singular			*plural*		
(yo)	**soy**	I am	(nosotros)	**somos**	we are
(tú)	**eres**	you are (informal)	(vosotros)	**sois**	you are
(él/ella)	**es**	he/she/it is	(ellos/ellas)	**son**	they are
(usted)	**es**	you are (formal	(ustedes)	**son**	you are (formal)

Use this verb for saying who you are and for describing permanent qualities.

Subject pronouns

Yo (I), **tú, usted** (you), **él** (he) etc. are *subject pronouns*. Because the ending of the verb shows who is the subject, you do not normally need to use these except to avoid ambiguity or to emphasize the subject.

How are you?/Where are you?

¿Como **estás?**   How are you?
Estoy muy bien. I am very well.

The second verb meaning "to be" is **estar**.
Here is the pattern of its endings:

estoy	I am	**estamos**	we are
estás	you are	**estáis**	you are
está	he/she is	**están**	they are
está	you are (formal)	**están**	you are (formal)

Use this verb for asking how someone is and for talking about where something or somebody is:

Aquí **está** Luisa.   Here is Luisa.
¿Dónde **están?**   Where are they?

My/your/his

There are several examples of these possessive adjectives in the Dialogues: **mi** esposa, **mi** hijo, **mi** hija, **tus** maletas, **tu** madre. The full list is as follows:

mi/mis	my	**nuestro(s)/nuestra(s)**	our
tu/tus	your (informal)	**vuestro(s)/vuestra(s)**	your (informal) (when talking to more than one person)
su/sus	your (formal); his/her/ its/their		

Note: The possessive adjective agrees in gender and number *with the word it accompanies*, not with the possessor.

Exclamations

¡Hola! Hello!   ¡Venga! Come here!   ¡Qué bien! How nice!

In written Spanish you always put an inverted exclamation mark at the beginning as well as the normal one at the end.

Asking questions and saying No

Asking a question is very simple. There are several alternative methods:

Question: ¿Es usted la señora Roberts? (subject pronoun after verb)
¿Usted es la señora Roberts? (same word order, rising intonation)
Usted es la señora Roberts, **¿verdad?** (no change of word order but add
      ¿verdad? or **¿no?** = isn't it? etc)
Statement: Sí, soy Carmen Roberts.

In written Spanish you always put an inverted question mark at the beginning of every question as well as the normal one at the end.
Negative statement: Insert **no** immediately before the verb.
No, **no** soy Carmen Roberts.   I am not Carmen Roberts.

things to do

1 Carmen is meeting a lot of people. Some of them she knows already:
José Machado, elderly business colleague of her husband:
Buenos días, señor. [She asks him how he is]
¿Cómo está usted?
  1 Mrs. Valbuena, wife of the journalist:
     [She says good morning and asks her how she is]
  2 Mr. Gómez, business contact:
     [She says good afternoon, and asks him how he is]
  3 Luis Ferrer, an old friend:
     [She says hello and asks him how he is]
     He says: Estoy muy bien, gracias, ¿y tú, cómo estás?
     [She says that she is well]
  4 Mari-Carmen Alfonso, her daughter's friend:
     [She says hello, good afternoon, and asks how things are]

2 Annie Rogers has arrived with her brother (**su hermano**) for a visit to a Spanish family. What does she say to the customs officer?
Aduanero: Su pasaporte, por favor. ¿Es usted la señorita Rogers?
Annie: . . . .
Aduanero: Este es su hermano, ¿verdad?
Annie: . . . .
Aduanero: ¿Es ésta su maleta?
Annie: . . . .
Aduanero: Y ¿ésta es la maleta de su hermano?
Annie: . . . .
Aduanero: Muy bien, señorita, gracias.

.3 Make up questions for the following answers:
  1 Sí, soy la señora Barillo.   **4** Estoy muy bien, gracias.
  2 No, no es mi maleta.   **5** Mi hermana se llama María Teresa.
  3 Está en la oficina.

MAKING CONVERSATION

¿cómo es tu casa?/what's your house like?

Juan plans to take Luisa and Miguel to their vacation house near Santander.

Luisa: ¿Dónde está tu casa?
Juan: **Está cerca de Santander.**
Luisa: ¿Cómo es la casa? ¿Es grande?
Juan: **No, es bastante pequeña.** Hay dos cuartos de dormir, un cuarto de estar, un comedor, una cocina moderna, un cuarto de baño y también hay una terraza y un jardín.
Luisa: ¿Está cerca del mar?
Juan: Sí, está muy cerca y hay una vista maravillosa de la playa.
Luisa: ¡Estupendo! **¿Y cuándo vamos?**
Juan: Pues, **¿vamos el miércoles?**
Luisa: De acuerdo. El miércoles está bien. ¿Vamos en tren?
Juan: Sí. Vamos en tren a Santander.

About the house

¿Dónde está tu casa?	Where is your house?
Está cerca de . . .	It's near . . .
¿Cómo es la casa?	What's the house like?
grande, pequeño/a	big, small
Hay/tiene	There is, there are/it has
dos dormitorios	two bedrooms
un cuarto de estar	a living room
un comedor	a dining room

una cocina moderna	a modern kitchen
un cuarto de baño	a bathroom
una terraza, un jardín	a terrace, a garden
Está muy cerca del mar.	It's very near the sea.
Hay una vista maravillosa de la playa.	There is a wonderful view of the beach.

Days of the week

¿Cuándo vamos?	When shall we go?
Vamos el miércoles.	We'll go on Wednesday.
El miércoles está bien.	Wednesday is fine.

OTHER USEFUL PHRASES

muy	very	también	too, also	De acuerdo.	Agreed, O.K.
bastante	quite, enough	¡Estupendo!	Great!	Vamos en tren.	We'll go by train.

ORDERING DRINKS AND SNACKS

Spanish bars   Spanish bars are crowded and friendly places and offer a wide variety of drinks and food. You can choose to stand at the counter (**la barra**) or sit at a table, or sometimes on the terrace (**terraza**), where you can watch the world go by but will pay a bit more. Although service will have been included, it is customary to give an extra tip (5%–10%) or at least to give some small change, if you are pleased with the service.

Many bars serve food as well. Often you will find rows of small dishes of appetizers (**tapas**) skewered with toothpicks laid out on the counter. If you want one of these, ask for **un pincho**. Larger portions are called **raciones**, and you will find there is often a huge variety to choose from.

vamos a tomar una copa/let's have a drink

Before supper the family decides to pay a visit to a nearby bar.

Camarero:	Buenas tardes, señores. ¿Qué van a tomar?
Carmen:	Miguel, tú, ¿qué tomas?
Miguel:	**Una coca-cola, por favor.**
Carmen:	**Y para mí un vermut.** Con hielo y limón, por favor. ¿Y tú, Luisa?
Luisa:	**Quiero** un zumo de naranja, por favor.
Camarero:	Sí, señorita.
Tom:	Yo quiero un vaso de vino tinto, por favor.
Camarero:	Muy bien, señores. ¿Quieren algo para comer?
Carmen:	**¿Qué tapas hay?**
Camarero:	Hay anchoas, aceitunas, calamares fritos, chorizo . . .
Carmen:	**Una ración de calamares** y una de aceitunas, por favor.
Camarero:	En seguida, señores.

Ordering drinks

¿Qué van a tomar, señores?	What will you have?
¿Quieren algo para comer?	Do you want anything to eat?
Hay anchoas, aceitunas, chorizo, calamares fritos . . .	We have anchovies, olives, garlic sausage, fried squid. . .
En seguida. . .	At once. . .
¿Qué tomas?	What'll you have?
Una coca-cola, por favor.	A coke, please.
Para mí un vermut	For me a vermouth
. . . con hielo y limón	. . . with ice and lemon
Quiero un zumo de naranja.	I want orange juice.
Yo quiero un vaso de vino tinto.	I'd like a glass of red wine.
Una cerveza, por favor.	A beer, please.
¿Qué tapas hay?	What appetizers do you have?

Las bebidas (drinks)

el vino tinto/ blanco/rosado	red/white/rosé/ wine
seco/dulce	dry/sweet
el jerez fino/amontillado/oloroso	dry/medium dry sweet sherry
la cerveza	lager, beer
. . . de barril	draft beer
la sangría	wine punch
el ginebra	gin
el vermut	vermouth
el cuba libre	rum and coke

Los refrescos (soft drinks)

el café, café solo	black coffee
café con leche	coffee with milk
la leche	milk
el agua	water
el té	tea
té con leche	tea with milk
el chocolate	chocolate
un batido	milkshake
una naranjada	orangeade
una limonada	lemonade
una gaseosa	fizzy drink

How to ask

Un tinto, por favor.	A red wine, please.	Un vaso de . . .	A glass of . . .
Una botella de . . .	A bottle of . . .	Un zumo de . . .	A . . . juice
Que esté bien frío	Nice and cold	. . . naranja/limón . . .	orange/lemon
Con hielo	With ice	Un taza de . . .	A cup of . . .
con gas/sin gas	carbonated/ noncarbonated	una coca-cola	coke

Las tapas (appetizers)

(Use **una ración de** when asking for a portion.)

salchichón	sausage	jamón serrano	cured ham
queso	cheese	gambas	prawns, shrimp
champiñones	mushrooms	mejillones	mussels
aceitunas	olives	anchoas	anchovies
cacahuetes	peanuts	almejas	clams
patatas fritas	potato chips	calamares	squid
tortilla española	Spanish omelette	pulpo	octopus
chorizo	spiced and seasoned pork sausage	sepia	cuttlefish

Snacks

Although **tapas** can be very substantial, if you want something even more filling you can buy many different kinds of carryout food. Street vendors sell **helados** (ice cream) and **churros** (long, thin sticks of fried batter dipped in sugar).

Los bocadillos (sandwiches made with French-type bread)

un bocadillo de queso/de jamón	a cheese/ham sandwich
de calamar/de tortilla	a squid/omelette sandwich
¿Qué bocadillos hay?	What sandwiches are there?
Uno de queso, por favor.	A cheese sandwich, please.

Other snacks

un sándwich (caliente)	toasted sandwich	¿Es para tomar ahora?	Is it to eat now?
una hamburguesa	hamburger	Para llevar	To go
un helado de vainilla/de fresa	a vanilla/strawberry ice cream		
de chocolate/de pistacho	a chocolate/pistachio ice cream		

the way it works

People and things

The word for "a" is **un** for masculine words and **una** for feminine words: e.g., **un** vaso (a glass), **una** casa (a house).

In the plural **un** becomes **unos** and **una** becomes **unas**: e.g., **un**os calamares (some squid), **un**as aceitunas (some olives).

There is, there are

Note the following expressions from the dialogue:
Hay dos cuartos de dormir. There are two bedrooms.
Hay una vista maravillosa. . . There is a wonderful view. . .
Hay is used in both singular and plural, and is the same in question form:
¿Qué tapas **hay**?   What tapas are there?

Describing people and places

Adjectives such as modern**o** (= modern), maravillos**a** (= wonderful), bonit**o** (= pretty) have **-o** and **-a** endings which change according to the gender of the word they accompany:

una cocin**a** modern**a**; una vist**a** maravillos**a** (feminine)
un cuart**o** bonit**o**; **un** cuart**o** modern**o** (masculine)
una casa viej**a** (an old house)
un jardín pequeñ**o** (a small garden)

Some adjectives, however, including grande (=big) and amable (= kind), do not change in the singular. *Note:* adjectives usually follow the noun.

With a plural word most adjectives add an **-s**: e.g., unos cuartos bonitos.

Going places

¿Cuándo **vamos**?   When do we go?
Vamos el miércoles.   We are going on Wednesday.

Vamos is part of the verb **ir** (to go). Here is the present tense:

voy	I go, am going	**vamos**	we go, are going
vas	you go, are going	**vais**	you go, are going
va	he/she/it goes, is going	**van**	they go, are going
	you go (formal)		you go (formal)

Saying what you want

One of the first things you need to say is "I want." You can do this simply by stating the object and adding "please": **Una coca-cola, por favor**. Or say:

Quiero una coca-cola. (from **querer**, to want)   I want a Coca-Cola.
Queremos unas tapas.   We want some tapas.

The complete pattern of the present tense of **querer** is as follows:

quiero	I want	**queremos**	we want
quieres	you want	**queréis**	you want
quiere	he/she wants	**quieren**	they want
	you want (formal)		you want (formal)

things to do

4 ¿**Cómo es tu casa?** Can you describe your own house or apartment? Use
some of the words on page 10: **moderno/viejo/bonito/grande/pequeño.**
1 ¿La casa? Es grande.   **4** ¿El cuarto de baño?
2 ¿El cuarto de estar?   **5** ¿El jardín?
3 ¿La cocina?   **6** ¿Tu cuarto de dormir? (*or* . . . dormitorio?)

5 You are in a café with a group of people. The waiter asks you what you
want: ¿**Qué quieren ustedes?**
You are the only person who can speak Spanish, so you do the talking . . .

Ann: [coffee with milk] Un café con leche, por favor.
Thomas: [a red wine]
Alice: [a cup of tea with lemon]
Isabel: [a beer]
Martin:

Now choose what you want yourself:
Y yo quiero . . .

6 It is time for a snack. First you go to a café-bar to buy a sandwich:
Camarero: ¿Qué va a tomar, señor/a?
You: [Ask what sandwiches there are]
Camarero: Hay de jamón, queso, chorizo, calamares . . .
You: [Say you'd like a ham sandwich, please]
Camarero: En seguida, señor/a.

Next you spot an ice cream stand . . .

You: [Ask what ice cream there is]
Ice cream vendor: Tengo vainilla, fresa, chocolate, limón, pistacho . . .
You: [Say you want a strawberry one, please]

7 Can you sort out which question goes with which answer?
1 ¿Qué tomas?	**(a)**	Está en el garaje.
2 ¿Cómo se llama la madre?	**(b)**	El domingo.
3 ¿Cómo es la casa?	**(c)**	Una cerveza, por favor.
4 ¿Dónde está el coche?	**(d)**	Es muy moderna.
5 ¿Cuándo vamos a la playa?	**(e)**	Se llama Caterina.

TALKING ABOUT ONESELF

¿de dónde es?/where are you from?

While Carmen is at work, Tom is arranging to rent a car for Thursday, and the manager is filling out a form and asking him some questions.

Gerente: Usted no es español, ¿verdad?

Tom: **No, no soy español, soy inglés.**

Gerente: Habla muy bien el español, señor.

Tom: Muchas gracias. **Pues mi esposa es española. Es de Santander.**

Gerente: ¿Es usted de Londres?

Tom: No, no soy de Londres. **Vivo en Southampton** pero **trabajo en Londres.**

Gerente: ¿En qué trabaja?

Tom: **Soy director de una empresa de computadoras.**

Gerente: ¿Está aquí de negocios?

Tom: No, yo estoy de vacaciones pero mi esposa está de negocios. **Es periodista.**

Gerente: ¿Y su dirección aquí en Madrid, por favor?

Tom: Es la calle del Duque de Sesto 72, tercer piso.

Gerente: Muy bien. **Tiene su permiso de conducir, ¿verdad?**

Tom: Sí. **Aquí tiene usted.**

Nationality and language

¿Es usted español/española?	Are you Spanish?
No, soy inglés/inglesa.	No, I'm English.
Soy alemán/americano.	I'm German/American.
Son canadienses/escocesas.	They are Canadian/Scottish.
Mi esposa es española.	My wife is Spanish.
Mi marido es español.	My husband is Spanish.
Hablo inglés.	I speak English.
¿Habla usted francés?	Do you speak French?
No hablo español.	I don't speak Spanish.
Hablo un poco de alemán.	I speak a little German.
Entiendo/No entiendo . . .	I understand/I don't understand. . .
Habla muy bien el español.	You speak Spanish very well.
Hable más despacio, por favor.	Speak more slowly, please.

Where are you from?

¿Es usted de Londres?	Are you from London?
Es de Santander.	She is from Santander.
Soy de Boston.	I am from Boston.
¿De dónde eres/es?	Where are you from?
¿Dónde vive usted? Vivo en . . .	Where do you live? I live in . . .
Su dirección, por favor.	Your address, please.

What do you do? *(See also list on p. 80.)*

¿En qué trabaja usted?	What is your job?
¿En qué trabajas?	What do you do for a living?
Soy director.	I am a director.
una empresa de computadoras	a computer firm
Trabajo en . . .	I work in . . .
¿Está aquí de negocios?	Are you here on business?
Estoy de vacaciones.	I am on vacation.
Es periodista.	She is a journalist.

Note: to say "I am a teacher," etc., in Spanish you say: **Soy profesor**, etc., without using the indefinite article.

Documents

Su pasaporte, por favor.	Your passport, please.
¿Tiene su permiso de conducir?	Do you have your driver's license?
Aquí tiene usted.	Here you are.

How old are you?

¿Cuántos años tiene/tienes?	How old is he/are you?
Tiene dos años.	He is two.
Tengo cuarenta y cinco años.	I'm 45.

Marital status

Soy casado/casada.	I am married.	Soy soltero/soltera.	I am single.

the way it works

Talking about yourself

When talking about yourself, your nationality, where you are from, what your profession is, etc., you always use the verb **ser**.

Soy inglés.	I am English.
Somos de Manhattan.	We are from Manhattan.
Es estudiante.	He is a student.

Verb groups

Note these expressions from the dialogues:

Habla muy bien el español.	You speak Spanish very well.
Trabajo en Londres.	I work in London.

These examples come from a group of regular Spanish verbs, the **-ar** group, so called because all the infinitives (or dictionary forms) end in **-ar**. The present tense of these verbs is as follows:

habl**ar**, *to speak*

habl-**o**	I speak	habl-**amos**	we speak
habl-**as**	you speak	habl-**áis**	you speak
habl-**a**	he/she speaks	habl-**an**	they speak
	you speak (formal)		you speak (formal)

There are two other verb groups, the **-er** group and the **-ir** group. Here is a regular example of the **-er** group:

beb**er**, *to drink*

beb-**o**	I drink	beb-**emos**	we drink
beb-**es**	you drink	beb-**éis**	you drink
beb-**e**	he/she drinks	beb-**en**	they drink
	you drink (formal)		you drink (formal)

and one of the **-ir** group:

viv**ir**, *to live*

viv-**o**	I live	viv-**imos**	we live
viv-**es**	you live	viv-**ís**	you live
viv-**e**	he/she lives	viv-**en**	they live
	you live (formal)		you live (formal)

Do you have . . . ? (¿Tiene . . . ?)

¿Tiene su permiso de conducir?	Do you have your driver's license?
Aquí **tiene** usted.	Here you are. (literally "you have it")

These phrases contain examples of the verb **tener** (to have), which is used very frequently. It conveys the idea of *possession* and *availability*. It is also used when talking about *age*:

¿Cuántos años **tienes**?	How old are you? (literally, "How many years do you have?")
Tengo 23 años.	I'm 23.

We will also meet **tener + que**, when it means "to have to":

Tengo que ir al dentista.	I have to go to the dentist.

Here is the complete pattern of the present tense of **tener**:

tengo	I have	**tenemos**	we have
tienes	you have	**tenéis**	you have
tiene	he/she/it has	**tienen**	they have
	you have (formal)		you have (formal)

things to do

1 **¿En qué trabajas?** (What do you do?) Can you sort out what everyone does by linking them with their place of work?

1 Soy	secretaria	Trabajo en	**(a)**	un hospital
2	profesor		**(b)**	una fábrica (factory)
3	enfermera		**(c)**	una tienda (shop)
4	mecánico		**(d)**	una oficina
5	ingeniero		**(e)**	un taller (garage)
6	dependienta		**(f)**	un colegio

2 You do it too! (Use **también** = too, also)
Example: Carmen habla español. Yo también hablo español.

1 Luisa habla inglés.
2 Juan estudia idiomas.
  (studies languages)
3 Tom trabaja en Londres.

4 Carmen y Tom hablan español.
Nosotros también . . .
5 Miguel y Luisa estudian español.
Nosotros también . . .

3 Can you describe your friend? Here are some useful words: **amable** (kind), **alto** (tall), **grande** (big), **bajo** (short), **simpático** (nice), **gordo** (fat), **guapa** (pretty).

You are asked to describe your Spanish friends to someone who wants to meet them. Here is the description of Miguel:

"Se llama Miguel. Miguel es inglés. Es de Londres. Habla español e inglés. Tiene 14 años. Es alto y delgado (= slim). Tiene una hermana que se llama Luisa."

1 Eduardo (from Madrid—accountant, aged 24—short and fat—one brother)
2 Can you describe yourself? *(See p. 80 for list of jobs.)*
  Me llamo . . . (your name)   Soy de . . . (where you are from)
  Vivo en . . . (where you live)   Soy . . . (what you do)
  Trabajo en . . . (where you work)   Tengo . . . (your age)

4 Everyone is telling you where they live.

1 Yo . . . en Madrid. ¿Dónde . . . usted?
2 Yo . . . en Tarragona, pero mi hermano . . . en Valencia.
3 Nosotros . . . en Toledo. Y vosotros, ¿dónde . . . ?
4 Y ellos, ¿dónde . . . ? ¿En Salamanca? No, . . . en Ciudad Real.

PUBLIC TRANSPORTATION

¿qué hora es?/what's the time?

Juan and Luisa are having lunch together. Juan has a sudden thought. . .

Juan: **¿Qué hora es, por favor?**
Luisa: Pues, **son las tres y media** . . .
Juan: ¡Hombre!¿**Son ya las tres y media?** ¡Me
        voy ahora mismo! Tengo una cita con el
        dentista a las cuatro y cuarto. **Adiós,
        hasta luego.**
Luisa: **Hasta luego.**

Telling the time

¿Qué hora es, por favor?	What time is it, please?
¿Son ya las tres y media?	Three-thirty already?
Me voy ahora mismo.	I must go/leave right now.
Tengo una cita con el dentista	I have a dentist appointment
a las cuatro y cuarto	at a quarter after four
antes/después	before/after

Saying goodbye

Adiós.	Goodbye.	**Hasta la vista.**	Till we meet again.
Hasta luego.	See you later.	**Hasta mañana.**	Till tomorrow.

Spanish trains   The Spanish National Rail Network is called **RENFE** (**Red Nacional de los Ferrocarriles Españoles**). There are many different kinds of trains, and variations in fares, so it is necessary to be specific when asking for information. Here is a list of the main trains:

el tranvía/ómnibus	slow train; makes every stop
el rápido	fast train; makes several stops
el expreso	long-distance night train; rather slow
el TALGO/TER	high-speed intercity express train

You pay a supplement to travel on many fast or long-distance trains. The cheapest days to travel are Blue Days (**Días Azules**) when, for long journeys, you can normally get a 20% reduction on individual round trip tickets. There are also other discounts available for families, groups, senior citizens, etc. Tickets bought in advance include a seat reservation, and you will therefore be asked what train you wish to take. Advance reservations are recommended, especially for intercity trains.

¿ a qué hora hay tren?/when is there a train?

When Juan returns he telephones the RENFE office (**la oficina de viajes RENFE**) to find out the times of the trains to Santander the next day.

Empleada:	Dígame.
Juan:	Buenos días. **¿A qué hora hay trenes para Santander**, por favor?
Empleada:	¿Cuándo quiere viajar?
Juan:	**Mañana por la mañana.**
Empleada:	**El Talgo sale a las ocho veinticinco** y hay un rápido a las once treinta.
Juan:	**¿A qué hora llega el Talgo a Santander?**
Empleada:	A las catorce cuarenta y cinco.
Juan:	**¿Hay que reservar asientos en el Talgo?**
Empleada:	Sí, señor.
Juan:	Gracias, señorita.
Empleada:	De nada. Adiós.

en el despacho de billetes/in the ticket office

The three go to the Chamartín Station to buy tickets for the next day.

Empleada:	¿Qué desean ustedes?
Juan:	**Tres billetes de segunda clase para Santander,** por favor.
Empleada:	Sí, señor. ¿De ida o de ida y vuelta?
Juan:	**De ida y vuelta.**
Empleada:	¿Para qué tren?
Juan:	**Para mañana, para el Talgo** de las ocho veinticinco.
Empleada:	Muy bien. Aquí tienen sus billetes.
Juan:	Gracias. **¿Cuánto es, por favor?**
Empleada:	Son doce mil treinta pesetas.
Juan:	Hay restaurante en el tren, ¿verdad?
Empleada:	Sí, señor.

Station notices

Estación de ferrocarril	Railway station
Trenes de cercanías	Local/suburban trains
Trenes de largo recorrido	Long-distance trains
Despacho de billetes	Ticket office
Llegadas/Salidas	Arrivals/Departures
Sala de espera/Consigna	Waiting room/Baggage claim
Horario/Destino	Timetable/Destination

Train information

la agencia de viajes	travel agency
la taquilla	ticket window
Venta anticipada	Sale of tickets in advance
¿A qué hora hay trenes para . . .?	At what time are there trains for . . .?
¿A qué hora sale . . .?	What time does . . . leave?
¿A qué hora es el próximo tren para . . .?	What time is the next train to . . .?
¿Cuándo quiere viajar?	When do you want to travel?
Mañana por la mañana	Tomorrow morning
El Talgo sale a . . .	The Talgo leaves at . . .
¿A qué hora llega . . .?	What time does it arrive?
¿Hay que reservar asientos?	Do you have to reserve seats?
¿Hay que pagar suplemento?	Do you have to pay a surcharge?
¿Hay restaurante/coche-cama?	Is there a dining car/sleeping car?
¿Hay coche-literas?	Are there berths?
¿De qué andén sale?	Which platform does it leave from?
Vía número tres	Platform three
¿Lleva retraso?	Is it late?
¿Cuánto tiempo tarda?	How long does it take?
fumador/no fumador	smoker/nonsmoker

Traveling by bus and coach   City buses are usually pay-as-you-enter and are run on a flat fare system. Before getting on the bus, check which number and route you want on the bus-stop sign. In Madrid, as well as the normal buses of the state-run **EMT (Empresa Municipal de Transportes)**, there are also privately run minibuses which are more expensive.

Intercity buses link Madrid with the provincial capitals and some villages and towns. Bus fares are fixed by the length of the journey, and on some long-distance routes, tickets are obtainable in advance.

Bus information
(see also train section above)

¿A qué hora hay autobús/autocar para . . .?	What time is there a local/intercity bus to . . .?
es el próximo autobús?	is the next bus?
es el último autobús?	is the last bus?
Hay uno a . . .	There's one at . . .
¿De dónde sale?	Where does it leave from?
Parada/Estación de autobuses	bus stop/station
plazas libres	seats free (available)
completo	full bus
Entrega de equipajes	Baggage check-in
Recogida de equipajes	Baggage claim (pick-up)

Buying a ticket

un billete	a ticket
Tres billetes para Santander	Three tickets to Santander
de segunda clase/de primera clase	second/first class
de ida/de ida y vuelta	one way/round trip
¿Para qué tren?	For which train?
No quedan billetes.	There are no tickets left.
Aquí tienen sus billetes.	Here are your tickets.
¿Cuánto es?	How much is it?
una reserva de asiento	a seat reservation
¿Hay reducciones para niños?	Are there discounts for children?
Sólo para menores de 12 años	Only for children under 12
¿Hay reducciones para estudiantes?	Are there student discounts?
una tarjeta familiar	a family ticket
un billete entero	one full-price ticket
un billete de niño	one child's ticket

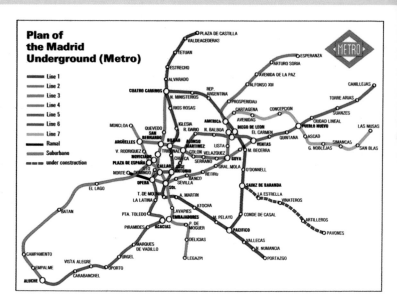

Plan of the Madrid Underground (Metro)

- ▬▬ Line 1
- ▬▬ Line 2
- ▬▬ Line 3
- ▬▬ Line 4
- ▬▬ Line 5
- ▬▬ Line 6
- ▬▬ Line 7
- ▬▬ Ramal
- ▬▬ Suburbano
- ▬ ▬ ▬ under construction

Listen for the following phrases

Vía número cuatro	Platform/Track number four
El tren con destino a . . .	The train for . . .
El tren procedente de . . .	The train from . . .

Traveling by metro   There are good subway or metro systems in Madrid and Barcelona, open from 5 am to 11 pm. Fares are inexpensive and are organized on a flat-fare basis. When you buy a ticket, check which line you want (**Línea**) and the name of the last station on the line (**Dirección**). To make a connection, look for the sign that says **Correspondencias**.

Metro (subway) travel

Uno, por favor.	One, please.
¿Qué línea es para . . .?	What line is for . . .?
La dos	Number two
¿Tengo que hacer transbordo?	Do I have to transfer?
No, es directo.	No, it's direct.
Sí, en Goya	Yes, at Goya station
Línea/Dirección	Line/direction
Correspondencia	Connection
Devuelve cambio	Change given
Precio exacto	Exact change/fare

SALIDA

BILLETES

Air travel information

¿A qué hora hay vuelos a Sevilla?	At what time are there flights to Seville?
¿Hay un vuelo a Londres hoy?	Is there a flight to London today?
Hay uno a las once de la mañana.	There's one at eleven in the morning.
Quisiera reservar un asiento.	I'd like to reserve a seat.
¿Es un vuelo directo?	Is it a direct flight?
¿Dónde está el terminal aéreo?	Where is the air terminal?

Taxis   Fares vary in different areas, but taxi drivers should have a list of approved fares for local runs. There is a basic initial charge, and additional surcharges will be added to the meter at night, on weekends, and on holidays.

Other notices

Parada de autobuses	Bus stop
Estación de autobuses	Bus station
Parada de taxis	Taxi stand
Oficina de Información	Information Office
Vuelos internacionales	International flights
Vuelos nacionales	Domestic flights
Salida	Exit

Asking and telling the time/¿Qué hora es?

To ask the time in Spanish use the verb ser: **¿Qué hora es?** What time is it?

The answer is either **Es la una** (*It's one o'clock*) or **Son las dos, tres,** etc. (*it's two, three o'clock*). (For numbers, see p. 79.)

Son las dos y cinco	It's 2:05	**Son las tres menos cinco**	It's 2:55
Son las dos y diez	It's 2:10	**Son las tres menos diez**	It's 2:50
Son las dos y cuarto	It's 2:15	**Son las tres menos cuarto**	It's 2:45
Son las dos y veinte	It's 2:20	**Son las tres menos veinte**	It's 2:40
Son las dos y veinticinco	It's 2:25	**Son las tres menos veinticinco**	It's 2:35
Son las dos y media	It's 2:30		

To say "am" and "pm" you say:

Son las diez de la mañana. It's 10:00 am.   A las cinco **de la tarde.** At 5 pm.
Son las diez de la noche. It's 10:00 pm.

24-hour clock

Official time in Spain is calculated on the 24-hour clock. So for train, bus, and air schedules, opening and closing times, etc., be prepared to hear, for example, the phrases on the following page.

El vuelo número IB367 con destino a Neuva York sale a las quince veinte.
El expreso sale de Madrid a las dieciocho veinte y llega a Murcia a las seis de la
mañana.

Note that the 24-hour clock leaves out **y** and **menos**: quince veinte = 15:20;
quince cincuenta = 15:50.

How to say "to" and "from," etc.

De is used to mean "of" or "from":

Sale **de** Madrid	It leaves *from* Madrid
las ocho **de** la mañana	8 o'clock *in (of)* the morning
de segunda clase	second class
la maleta **de** Luisa	Luisa's suitcase (suitcase *of* Luisa)

A means "at" or "to":

¿**A** qué hora?	*At* what time?
Voy **a** Santander	I'm going *to* Santander
Llega **a** Santander	It arrives *at* Santander
a las diecinueve cuarenta	*at* 19:40

Another useful word in this dialogue is **para**, which means "for."

los trenes **para** Santander	the trains *for* Santander (para = destination)
para dos personas	*for* two people
para hoy/**para** mañana	*for* today/*for* tomorrow BUT
por la mañana	*in* the morning (por = *during*)

It leaves at ten

Sale a las ocho veinticinco.	It leaves at 8:25. (from **salir**)
Llega a las catorce.	It arrives at 14:00. (from **llegar**)

You will find both these verbs are very useful. While **llegar** is a regular **-ar** verb
(like **trabajar**), **salir** is an **-ir** verb with an irregular first person form:

salgo	I leave	**salimos**	we leave
sales	you leave	**salís**	you leave
sale	he/she/it leaves	**salen**	they leave
	you leave (formal)		you leave (formal)

things to do

2.5 ¿Qué hora es? You are with a group of people and someone stops you
to ask the time. The trouble is that everyone's watch says something
different! **Son las . . .**

6 ¿A qué hora hay autobús para Segovia?

Destino	Salida	Destino	Salida
Segovia	10:15	Badajoz	5:45
Ávila	15:30	Huelva	9:30
Valladolid	10:35	Toledo	11:25

Can you say what time the buses run:
¿A qué hora hay autobús para Segovia?   Hay uno a las diez y cuarto.

1 ¿A qué hora hay autobús para Toledo? **4** ¿A qué hora hay autobús
2 ¿A qué hora hay autobús para Ávila?   para Huelva?
3 ¿A qué hora hay autobús para Badajoz? **5** ¿A qué hora hay autobús
                                             para Valladolid?

7 Look at the price information sheet and answer:

	Ida	**Ida y vuelta**
Madrid-Santander	3.700 ptas	5.000 ptas
Madrid-Barcelona	4.200 ptas	7.500 ptas
Madrid-Torremolinos	4.500 ptas	6.200 ptas

1 Quiero un billete de ida para Santander. ¿Cuánto es? Son . . .
2 Quiero un billete de ida y vuelta para Barcelona. ¿Cuánto es? Son . . .
3 Quiero un billete de ida para Torremolinos. ¿Cuánto es? Son . . .

8 *(a)* You overhear the ticket agent advising a passenger about trains. Can
you guess what the passenger is asking?

Passenger: ¿ . . . . ?
Agent: El próximo tren para Sevilla sale a las nueve doce.
Passenger: ¿ . . . . ?
Agent: Llega a las quince treinta.

(b) **En el metro.** Juan wants to go to Colón station for his dentist
appointment. Can you fill in his part of the conversation?

Juan: [One, please]
Agent: Aquí tiene. Ciento ochenta pesetas.
Juan: [Ask what line is for Colón]
Agent: Es la cuatro.
Juan: [Ask if you have to transfer]
Agent: No, es directo.

SHOPPING

▶ ▶ ▶ **Shopping** Most shops in Spain close for a few hours in the early afternoon. Shops are usually open from 9:30 am to 1:30 pm and from 4:00 pm to 8:00 pm. Many shops are closed on Sundays, although they may remain open in the summer and around the Christmas holiday. As in America, department stores sell a wide range of goods such as furniture (**muebles**), clothes (**ropa**), and gifts (**regalos**). Major credit cards (**tarjetas de crédito**) are accepted in most large stores and in many smaller shops.

los grandes almacenes/the department store

Carmen wants to buy a leather jacket and she goes to the Nuevas Galerías (a big department store). There she talks to a sales clerk.

Dependienta:	¿Qué desea, señora?
Carmen:	**Quisiera una chaqueta de cuero.**
Dependienta:	¿Es para usted? ¿Cuál es su talla?
Carmen:	**La cuarenta y dos.**
Dependienta:	(shows her some) ¿Le gusta este estilo? Tenemos en negro, marrón y azul oscuro.
Carmen:	Sí, **el estilo me gusta, pero no me gusta el color.** Me gusta más la negra—es más elegante. **¿Puedo probármela?**
Dependienta:	Sí, señora. Pase por aquí, por favor.

(Carmen tries it on but finds it too small.)

Carmen:	¡Qué lástima! No me sienta bien. **Es demasiado pequeña.** ¿Me puede enseñar otra más grande?
Dependienta:	Claro, señora, aquí está. (she tries it on) ¿Qué le parece?
Carmen:	Sí, me parece muy bien. **¿Cuánto cuesta, por favor?**
Dependienta:	Cuesta diez mil quinientas pesetas.
Carmen:	Bueno, **me la quedo.**

Shopping—clothes and accessories

¿Qué desea, señora?	What do you want, ma'am?
¿Es para usted?	Is it for you?
¿Cuál es su talla?	What is your size?
¿Qué número tiene?	What size do you wear? (shoes)
¿Le gusta este estilo/color?	Do you like this style/color?
Tenemos en negro/en marrón/en azul	We have it in black/brown/blue
Los probadores están allí.	The fitting rooms are over there.
Pase por aquí, por favor.	Come this way, please.
¿Algo más?	Anything else?
Lo siento.	I'm sorry.
Es el/la más barato/a que tenemos.	It is the cheapest one we have.
Sólo quiero mirar.	I'm just looking.
Quiero/Quisiera . . .	I want/I'd like . . .
una chaqueta de cuero	a leather jacket
(Mi talla) es la cuarenta y dos.	(My size) is a 42.
Mi número es . . .	My size is . . . (shoes)
Me gusta/no me gusta	I like it/I don't like it
el color/el estilo	the color/the style
¿Tiene algo en rojo/verde?	Do you have anything in red/green?
Me gusta más . . .	I prefer . . .
la negra	the black one
Es más elegante.	It's more elegant.
Me gusta mucho.	I like it very much.
¿Puedo probármelo/probármela?	Can I try it on?
Me sienta bien (no me sienta).	It fits me (doesn't fit me).
Es demasiado pequeño/a, grande, corto/a, largo/a, caro/a	It's too small, big, short, long, expensive
¿Hay otro más grande?/más barato?	Is there a bigger one?/cheaper one?
¿Me puede enseñar otro/a . . .?	Can you show me another . . .?
¿Cuánto cuesta?	How much does it cost?
Me lo quedo/me la quedo.	I'll take it.
Lo/la compro.	I'll buy it.

USEFUL WORDS AND PHRASES

¿Qué le parece?	What do you think?
Me parece muy bien.	I think it's fine.
¡Qué lástima!	What a pity!
OFERTA/REBAJAS	SALE/BARGAINS

Clothes sizes—women									
American	4	6	8	10	12	14	16		
Spanish	38	40	42	44	46	48	50		

Collar sizes—men (approximate)									
American	14	14½	15	15½	16	16½	17		
Spanish	36	37	38	39/40	41	42	43		

Shoe sizes									
American	5	6	7	8	9	10	11	12	13	14
Spanish	35	36	37	38	39	40	41	42	43	44

en el estanco/at the tobacconist's

In Spain you do not normally need to go to the post office to buy stamps— you can buy them in an **estanco** (a tobacco shop) which usually sells postcards and stamps as well as tobacco and cigarettes (**cigarrillos**), and sometimes newspapers as well. Tom is choosing some postcards, but he is unlucky with the stamps. . .

Tom: **Quiero estas cuatro postales, por favor.**
Dependiente: Sí, señor. Las postales cuestan quince pesetas.
Tom: Y, **¿tiene usted sellos?** Quiero cuatro para Inglaterra.
Dependiente: No, señor. **Tiene que ir a Correos. ¿Algo más?**
Tom: ¿Tiene periódicos ingleses?
Dependiente: Me parece que tengo uno . . . Pero no lo veo. Lo siento, señor, no queda ninguno. Hay un quiosco en la esquina.
Tom: Gracias, entonces, **eso es todo.**

Buying postcards and stamps

Quiero estas cuatro postales.	I want these four postcards.
¿Tiene usted sellos?	Do you have stamps?
Cuatro para los Estados Unidos.	Four for the United States.
Tiene que ir a Correos.	You'll have to go to the post office.
¿Algo más?	Anything else?
¿Tiene usted periódicos/revistas ingleses/-as?	Do you have English newspapers/ magazines?
Me parece que tengo uno.	I think I have one.
Pero no lo veo.	But I don't see it.

No me queda ninguno.	I have none left.
Hay un quiosco en la esquina.	There's a newsstand on the corner.
Eso es todo.	That's all.

the way it works

This and that

The word for "this" is **este** for masculine nouns and **esta** for feminine nouns:

este estilo	this style		**esta** chaqueta	this jacket

To say "that" you normally use **ese, esa**:

ese color	that color		**esa** camisa	that shirt

In the plural the pattern is as follows:

est**os**, est**as**	these	**esos, esas**	those

To say "this one" or "that one" use **éste, ésta** or **ése, ésa** with an accent. In a less specific sense **esto, eso** can also mean "this" and "that."

More or less

The word for "more" is **más** and "less" is **menos**: **más grande** (bigger); **más pequeño** (smaller); **más caro** (more expensive); **más barato** (cheaper). To say "bigger than" or "more . . . than" you use **más . . . que**.

Este traje es **más grande que** el otro. (bigger than the other)
Esta camisa es **más cara que** la otra. (more expensive than the other)

If you want to say "biggest" or "the most . . ." you can use **el/la más**:

Esta camisa es **la más grande**. (the biggest)
Este vestido es **el más barato**. (the cheapest)

Object pronouns

(1) Direct

¿El periódico? No **lo** veo.	The newspaper? I don't see it.
¿La chaqueta? **La** compro.	The jacket? I'll buy it.
¿Los zapatos? Me **los** quedo.	The shoes? I'll take them.
¿Las postales? No **las** veo.	The postcards? I don't see them.

As well as *it* and *them* we sometimes use a person as the object, e.g., *me* or *you*:

La conozco/**las** conozco	I know her/them (fem.)
Le veo/**les** veo	I see him/them (masc.)
Me ve/**te** ve	He sees me/he sees you

Here is a list of direct object pronouns:

me	me	nos	us
te	you	os	you
le/la	him, her	les/las	them (people)
	you (masc./fem.)		you (masc./fem.)
lo/la	it (masc./fem.)	los/las	them (things)

(2) Indirect

¿**Me** puede enseñar otro?	Can you show *(to) me* another one?
¿Qué **le** parece?	How does it seem *to you*?

Here is a list of indirect object pronouns:

me	to me	nos	to us
te	to you	os	to you
le	to him/her	les	to them (people)
	to you		to you
le	to it	les	to them (things)

Note that the object pronoun normally comes *before* the verb. When the verb is in the infinitive, however, the object pronoun may either precede or follow, in which case it is added on to the infinitive itself: ¿Puedo **probármela**? (Can I try it on?).

How to say "I like it"

Look at the following phrases taken from the dialogues:

¿Le gusta este estilo?	Do you like this style?
Sí, me gusta.	Yes, I like it.
No me gusta el color.	I don't like the color.
Me gusta más . . .	I prefer . . .
Me gusta mucho.	I like it very much.

From these examples you can see that the word "like" is used in a different way from English. **Me gusta el estilo** (I like the style) really means "the style is pleasing to me" (indirect object). With more than one thing use gust**an**.

Me gustan estas camisas.	I like these shirts.

Here is the verb in full:

me gusta(n)	I like	nos gusta(n)	we like
te gusta(n)	you like	os gusta(n)	you like
le gusta(n)	he/she likes	les gusta(n)	they like
le gusta(n)	you like (formal)	les gusta(n)	you like (formal)

things to do

3.1 Carmen is describing to her sister some of the clothes she has seen. For colors and materials, see p. 80.

1 Q. ¿El vestido (*dress*) es rojo y negro?
   A. Sí, es rojo y negro.
2 Q. ¿La falda (*skirt*) es verde?
3 Q. ¿La camisa (*shirt*) es amarilla?
      Y, ¿es de seda o de algodón?
4 Q. ¿ El suéter es marrón?
      Y, ¿es de lana o de acrílico?
5 Q. ¿Los pantalones son grises?

You are in a department store buying a tee-shirt (**una camiseta**). Can you fill in your part of the conversation?

Clerk: ¿Qué desea, señorita?
You: [Say you want a tee-shirt]
Clerk: ¿Qué talla tiene?
You: [Say you take a 44]
Clerk: ¿Le gusta ésta?
You: [Say you like the style but not the color]
Clerk: La tenemos también en rojo y en azul.
You: [Say you prefer the blue. Ask if you can try it on]
Clerk: ¿Qué le parece, señorita?
You: [Say you like it and ask how much it is]
Clerk: Cuesta mil ochocientas cuarenta pesetas.
You: [Say you'll buy it]

See how difficult it is to get a good fit!

Clerk: ¿Le gusta este traje?
You: No, es demasiado . . . ¿Hay otro más . . .?

Clerk: ¿Le gusta esta camisa?
You: . . . .
Clerk: ¿Le gusta este sombrero?
You: . . . .
Clerk: ¿Le gustan estos vaqueros?
You: Son . . . . ¿Hay otros más . . .?
Clerk: ¿Le gustan estos zapatos?
You: . . . .

¿Cuánto cuesta? Can you say the prices of these articles in Spanish?

Tienes que ir a la librería. Can you match the following items with the shops where you can buy them? (See p. 81 for a list of shops.)

1 una pila (battery)   (a) la ferretería
2 un diccionario (dictionary)   (b) el quiosco
3 un perfume   (c) la tienda de aparatos eléctricos
4 un periódico (newspaper)   (d) la perfumería
5 un sacacorchos (corkscrew)   (e) la papelería
6 un mapa (map)   (f) la librería

BUYING FOOD

▶ ▶ ▶ **Food shops**   There are several names for a grocery store in Spain—
tienda de comestibles, alimentación, tienda de ultramarinos. You
can, of course, also buy food in the market (**mercado**) and supermarket
(**supermercado**), and there are also increasing numbers of hypermarkets
(**hipermercados**), oversized stores for food, clothing, and a wide variety of
goods.

en la tienda de comestibles/at the grocery store

Juan, Luisa, and Miguel have arrived in Santander and are stocking up on
groceries.

Luisa: Mantequilla, leche, galletas, anchoas y frutas.
Dependiente: Buenos días, señorita. ¿Qué desea?
Luisa: **Deme doscientos gramos de jamón . . ., medio kilo
                de** salchichas . . ., **cien gramos de** chorizo . . ., medio
                kilo de este queso manchego . . ., cien gramos de
                mantequilla . . ., y **un litro de** leche, por favor.
Dependiente: ¿Algo más, señorita?
Luisa: Sí. **Póngame un paquete de** esas galletas, y una lata
                de anchoas . . ., y **un kilo de** manzanas . . . Y ya está.
Miguel: Oye, Luisa, mira estos melocotones. Me gustan
                muchísimo los melocotones y están bien maduros. ¿Qué
                te parece?

Luisa:	Bueno, chico, **vamos a comprar medio kilo de** melocotones para ti. Y eso es todo. ¿Cuánto es, por favor?
Dependiente:	Son novecientas sesenta y cinco pesetas en total, señorita.
Luisa:	Vale. (hands him the money) ¿Tiene una bolsa de plástico, por favor?
Dependiente:	Aquí tiene. Adiós, señorita.

Shopping—food

¿Qué tenemos que comprar?	What do we have to buy?
Deme doscientos gramos de . . .	Give me 200 grams of . . .
este queso manchego	this cheese from La Mancha
. . . medio kilo de jamón	. . . half a kilo of ham
. . . cuarto de kilo de salchichón/ salchichas	. . . quarter of a kilo of (large) sausage/sausages
. . . cien gramos de mantequilla	. . . 100 grams of butter
. . . un litro de leche	. . . 1 liter of milk
¿Algo más?	Anything else?
Póngame un paquete de . . .	Give me a packet (package) of
esas galletas	those crackers (cookies)
. . . una lata de anchoas	. . . a can of anchovies
. . . un kilo de manzanas	. . . a kilo of apples
una rodaja de . . .	a slice of . . .
un trozo de . . .	a piece of . . .
Y ya está.	And that's it.
estos melocotones	these peaches
Me gusta(n) muchísimo . . .	I adore . . .
Está(n) bien maduro(s).	It is/They are nice and ripe.
¿Qué te parece?	What do you think?
Vamos a comprar . . .	We'll buy . . .
¿Cuánto es, por favor?	How much is it, please?
Son novecientas sesenta y cinco ptas	That's 965 pesetas
Vale	O.K.
¿Tiene una bolsa de plástico?	Do you have a plastic bag?
Aquí tiene.	Here you are.
Congelados	Frozen food
un poco más/menos	a little more/less
bastante/demasiado	enough/too much

GOING TO THE BANK

Banks and currency exchanges   Banking hours are from 9 am to 2 pm on Monday to Friday and from 9 am to 1 pm on Saturday. You can change money in some shops and hotels (look for the **Cambio** sign) as well as in banks, but you will get a better rate of exchange in a bank. ATMs are a convenient way to withdraw money while traveling in Spain. ATMs are prevalent in large cities such as Madrid, as well as smaller towns throughout the country.

en el banco/in the bank

En el banco/at the bank

Tom goes to the bank to cash some traveler's checks:

Tom:	Buenos días. **Quisiera cambiar unos cheques de viajero, por favor.**
Empleada:	Sí, señor. ¿Cuánto quiere cambiar?
Tom:	Cien libras. **¿A cómo está el cambio hoy?**
Empleada:	A ciento noventa y seis pesetas. ¿Su pasaporte, por favor? . . . Firme usted aquí. . . . ¿Quiere pasar a la caja, por favor?
Cajero:	¿Cómo quiere su dinero, señor?
Tom:	Pues, **deme tres billetes de cinco mil pesetas** y el resto en billetes de menor valor.

Money language

Cambio	Exchange
Quisiera cambiar . . .	I'd like to change . . .
unos cheques de viaje/ viajero	some traveler's checks
unas libras esterlinas	some pounds sterling
unos dólares	some dollars
¿Cuánto quiere cambiar?	How much do you want to change?
Cien dólares	$100
¿A cómo está el cambio?	What is the exchange rate?
A ciento noventa y seis	196 pesetas
Firme usted aquí.	Sign here.
¿Quiere pasar a la caja?	Please go to the cashier.
¿Cómo quiere su dinero?	How do you want your money?
Deme tres billetes.	Give me three bills.
el resto	the rest
menor valor	lesser value
¿Puede darme cambio?	Can you give me change?
las monedas	coins
los eurocheques	Eurocheques
la tarjeta de crédito	credit card
la carta de crédito	letter of credit
Quiero abrir una cuenta	I want to open an account
acreditar esto	to credit this

the way it works

Asking how much

There are several ways to ask the price of things. Here Luisa uses:

¿Cuánto es?	How much is it?

You will also hear:

¿Cuánto cuesta/n?   How much is it/are they?
¿Cuánto vale/valen?   How much is it/are they (worth)?

In the bank Tom asks the exchange rate:

¿A cómo está el cambio?   What is the exchange rate?

We'll buy half a kilo/Vamos a comprar medio kilo.

The useful phrase **voy a . . . + infinitive** is the simplest way of expressing the future tense:

Vamos a tomar una copa.   We'll have a drink.
Voy a ver.   I'll go and see.
¿Qué **van a** tomar?   What will you have (to eat/drink)?

things to do

Your friend has a long shopping list. Can you tell him where to go for each item? (See also list on p. 81.)

1 el pan	(a) la pastelería
2 la carne	(b) la tienda de comestibles
3 las naranjas	(c) la pescadería
4 la leche	(d) la frutería
5 el azúcar	(e) la panadería
6 el pescado	(f) la tienda de vinos
7 el vino	(g) la lechería
8 un pastel	(h) la carnicería

This is your shopping list. Can you ask for each item in turn? (for numbers see p. 79)

250g butter
1 litre milk
500g ham
1 packet biscuits
1 tin sardines
1 kilo bananas
½ kilo peaches
6 pears
1 litre oil
2 bottles red wine
12 eggs

Start by saying: Quiero . . . Deme . . . Póngame . . .

3.8 How much does it all cost? ¿Cuánto es todo?

Work out how much the following will cost you per item, and then give the total: **un paquete de café; una docena de huevos; medio kilo de plátanos; dos kilos de tomates.**

3.9 You are in a **tienda de comestibles** buying various items.

Shopkeeper:	Hola, buenos días.
You:	[Say you want 200 grams of cheese and 100 grams of ham]
Shopkeeper:	¿Y algo más?
You:	[Ask for half a kilo of apples and 6 ripe bananas]
Shopkeeper:	Muy bien. ¿Algo más?
You:	[Ask for a liter of milk. Say that's all and ask how much]

3.10 You are in a bank and you want to change some money.

You:	[Say good morning. You want to change some dollars]
Clerk:	¿Cuánto quiere cambiar?
You:	[$150. Ask what the exchange rate is]
Clerk:	A noventa pesetas. Firme aquí, por favor, y pase a la caja.
Cashier:	¿Cómo quiere su dinero?
You:	[Say you want two 5,000 peseta bills, three 1,000 bills, and one 500 bill]

3.11 You are in a **pastelería** and your mouth is watering! (See list on p. 82.)

Señora:	¿Puedo ayudarle?
You:	[Say you'd like two of those cakes and a tart]
Señora:	¿Algo más?
You:	[Say yes, ask her to give you a doughnut and bread roll]
Señora:	¿Es para tomar ahora?
You:	[No, it's to go]

FINDING YOUR WAY

La Oficina de Turismo Most Spanish towns have a tourist office, which is usually the best place to obtain local maps and information about the region.

¿cómo puedo llegar a …/how do I get to …?

Luisa and Miguel are trying to find their way around in Santander.

Luisa:	¿Dónde está la Oficina de Turismo, por favor?
Passerby:	No está lejos. Van a pie, ¿verdad?
Luisa:	Si está cerca, vamos a pie.
Passerby:	Pues, **tomen la primera calle a la derecha** y **sigan todo derecho.** Al final de esa calle llegan ustedes a la plaza. Está en la plaza **a la izquierda** enfrente de la Catedral.
Luisa:	Gracias, señor. ¿Y **hay un banco por aquí,** por favor?
Passerby:	Sí, señorita. Hay muchos bancos. **Cojan la segunda calle a la derecha.** Hay un banco en la esquina al lado de la biblioteca.

35

Miguel:	¿No **se puede coger un autobús?**
Luisa:	¡Qué perezoso eres! No, vamos andando. El banco está a unos diez minutos, nada más. Gracias, señor.
Passerby:	De nada, adiós.

Tom is driving to Ávila with Carmen. He is not
quite sure of the way out of Madrid.

Tom:	**Perdón, ¿la carretera de Ávila, por favor?**
Policeman:	Pues, siga hasta el final de esta calle y doble a la derecha. Tome la segunda calle a la izquierda y allí está la carretera. Se llama la Calle de la Princesa.
Tom:	Gracias.

Asking the way

¿Dónde está la Oficina de Turismo?	Where is the tourist office?
No está lejos.	It's not far away.
¿Van a pie?	Are you going on foot?
Si está cerca.	If it's near.
Tome(n) la primera calle	Take the first street
a la derecha/a la izquierda	on the right/on the left
siga(n) todo derecho/recto	continue straight ahead
llegan ustedes	you'll arrive
a la plaza	in the square
enfrente de la Catedral	opposite the Cathedral
¿Hay un banco por aquí?	Is there a bank near here?
Hay muchos bancos.	There are many banks.
Coja la segunda calle	Take the second street
en la esquina	on the corner
al lado de la biblioteca	beside the library
¿No se puede coger un autobús?	Can't one take a bus?
Hay que coger un autobús.	You must take a bus.
Vamos andando/en coche/en autobús/ en taxi/en bicicleta/en motocicleta	We'll go on foot/by car/by bus/ by taxi/bike/motorcycle
Está a unos diez minutos.	It's about ten minutes (walk).
¿La carretera de Ávila?	The road to Ávila?
Siga hasta el final de esta avenida	Go to the end of this avenue
Doble a la derecha	Turn right
¿Cómo puedo llegar a . . .?	How can I get to . . .?
la parada está allí enfrente	The bus stop is opposite
Cambie de autobús	Change buses

OTHER USEFUL PHRASES

¡Qué perezoso eres!	What a lazybones you are!
Perdón	Excuse me
¿Tiene un mapa de la ciudad?	Do you have a map of the city?

**OFICINA
DE
TURISMO**

the way it works

Asking for directions

There are several ways to ask for directions.

¿La Catedral, **por favor?**	The Cathedral, *please?*
¿**Dónde está** la estación?	*Where is* the station?
¿**Por dónde se va a** la playa?	*How do you get to* the beach?
¿**Cómo puedo llegar al** albergue de juventud?	*How can I get to* the youth hostel?
¿**Para ir a** la playa?	*To get to* the beach?
¿**Hay** un banco **por aquí?**	*Is there* a bank *near here?*

Understanding instructions

Not only might you have to ask the way, but you will also have to be able to understand the various ways in which instructions are given in Spanish. Look at the following phrases:

Tomen la primera calle . . . **sigan** todo derecho . . . **Coja** la segunda calle . . . **Doble** a la derecha . . . **Tome** el número dos . . . **Cambie** de autobús

These forms of the verbs are known as the imperative (or command). The imperative is formed by taking the stem of the first person ("I" form) of the present tense (e.g., **tom-o, coj-o, sig-o**) and adding the following sets of endings:

For **-ar** verbs, e.g., **tomar** (to take) add **-e** (sing.), **-en** (pl.): **tome, tomen; doble, doblen.**
For **-er** and **-ir** verbs, e.g., **seguir** (to follow), **subir** (to go up) add **-a** (sing.), **-an** (pl.): **siga, sigan; suba, suban.**

Note: the verb **ir** (to go) is irregular, the imperative being **vaya** (sing.) and **vayan** (pl.).

Methods of transportation

Note the different ways of getting around: Vamos **a pie, en tren, en coche, en avión,** etc.
The verb **coger** is used for "to catch" or "take": "To get on (a bus)" is **subir** and "to get off" is **bajar: Subes** a la estación y **bajas** a la playa (You get on at the station and get off at the beach).

Place and distance words

The following expressions are essential for giving directions and it is worth listening for them:

a la derecha	to/on the right	al lado (de)	beside, next to
a la izquierda	to/on the left	en la esquina	on the corner
todo derecho	straight ahead	al final (de)	at the end (of)
cerca (de)	near (to)	allí	there
lejos (de)	far (from)	aquí	here
aquí mismo	right here	enfrente (de)	opposite, in front (of)
hacia	towards	hasta	until, up to
por	along	por aquí	hereabouts, around here
detrás (de)	behind	delante (de)	in front (of)
al otro lado	on the other side		

Notice the use of **primero, segundo,** etc.

la primera calle a la derecha   the first street on the right
la segunda calle a la izquierda   the second street on the left

Also, you may be told how long it will take to get to your destination:

Está **a unos quince minutos.**   It's about fifteen minutes away.
Está **a una hora de viaje** de aquí. It's an hour's journey from here.

and the distance:

Está **a doscientos metros.**   It's 200 meters away.
Está **a cien kilómetros.**   It's 100 kilometers away.

Poder (to be able) and volver (to return)

Some Spanish verbs change not only their endings but also the middle of the word. In the case of both these **-er** verbs there is a vowel change from **o** to **ue** in the stem of the 1st, 2nd and 3rd persons singular and 3rd plural.

p**ue**do	I can	p**o**demos	we can
p**ue**des	you can (fam.)	p**o**déis	you can (fam.)
p**ue**de	he/she/you can	p**ue**den	they/you can
v**ue**lvo	I return	v**o**lvemos	we return
v**ue**lves	you return (fam.)	v**o**lvéis	you return (fam.)
v**ue**lve	he/she returns, you return	v**ue**lven	they/you return

Impersonal se

To say ''Can one do this?'' or ''How do you get to . . .?'' Spanish uses an impersonal pronoun **se** which is the equivalent of *one, you, they*, etc. before the third person of the verb:

¿Por dónde **se va** a la playa?   How does one get to the beach?
¿**Se puede** aparcar aquí?   Can you park here?
¿Dónde **se puede** comprar el pan?   Where can one buy bread?
¿No **se puede** coger un taxi?   Can't we take a taxi?

The answer is formed in exactly the same way, namely:

Se va por la plaza.   One goes through the square.
Sí, **se puede.**/No, **no se puede.**   Yes, you can./No, you can't.

things to do

4.1 Can you work out how to get there? Follow the example.
¿Por dónde se va a la catedral? ⊢→ Tome la primera calle a la derecha.

1 ¿ . . . a la iglesia? (church) ←⊣   **3** ¿ . . . al parque? (park) ↑

2 ¿ . . . al museo? (museum) ⊢→   **4** ¿ . . . a la plaza? (square) ⌐↑

You are in the Calle de Castilla, by the station. (☆ marks the spot.) Look at the map and find out where you are being directed to:

1 Tome la primera calle a la izquierda y luego la segunda a la derecha y siga todo derecho. Está a la izquierda.

2 Tome la tercera calle a la izquierda que se llama la Calle de la Lealtad y luego la primera a la derecha. Está allí en la plaza, enfrente de la Catedral.

3 Pase por delante de la Catedral hasta la Plaza Porticada. Está allí a la izquierda.

4 Tome la primera calle a la derecha y en seguida doble a la derecha otra vez. Está a la derecha en la esquina.

5 Coja la primera calle a la izquierda y al final de esa calle tome la calle a la izquierda que se llama la Calle Alta. Siga todo derecho hasta el final y está allí a la izquierda.

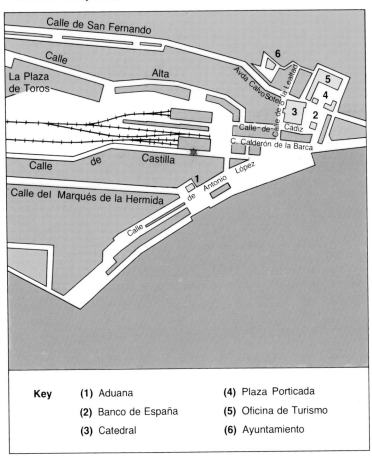

Key

(1) Aduana
(2) Banco de España
(3) Catedral
(4) Plaza Porticada
(5) Oficina de Turismo
(6) Ayuntamiento

DRIVING AND BREAKDOWNS

▶ ▶ ▶ **Driving**   An International Driver's License (or an authorized translation of your American license) is recommended, and you must have your license with you. It is compulsory to have your registration and adequate insurance. Spain adheres to the International Highway Code. Speed limits are normally:

Freeways (**autopistas = A**)	120 km/h (75 mph)
National Highways (**carreteras nacionales = N**)	100 km/h (62 mph)
Other roads	90 km/h (56 mph)
Residential areas	60 km/h (37 mph)

Gas stations are relatively infrequent outside the main towns, so it's advisable to fill up when you have an opportunity. There are two main grades of gas: **super** (97 octane) and **normal** (92 octane). You cannot always use your credit card. On most freeways a toll (**peaje**) is payable, the amount depending on the distance covered. Wearing a seatbelt (**cinturón de seguridad**) is compulsory.

en la gasolinera/at the gas station

Tom and Carmen are in the car driving to Ávila. They stop to buy gas.

Empleada:	Buenas tardes, señor.
Tom:	Buenas tardes. **Lleno de super, por favor.**
Empleada:	Bueno. Ya está, cuarenta y ocho litros.
Tom:	**¿Quiere comprobar el aceite y el agua,** por favor?
Empleada:	(Checks oil and water) Necesita medio litro de aceite.
Tom:	Muchas gracias. ¿Cuánto le debo?
Empleada:	Son cuatro mil trescientas pesetas.

el taller mecánico/the garage

Unfortunately, after setting off again, they have a flat tire and after changing the tire, they stop in at a garage on the outskirts of Ávila.

Tom:	Hola, buenas tardes. Tengo un problema con el neumático. **¿Puede repararlo, por favor?**
Empleado:	Bueno, vamos a ver . . . Tiene un agujero bastante grande, pero creo que puedo hacerlo. ¿Puede volver dentro de un rato?
Tom:	Muy bien. Vuelvo en veinte minutos, ¿verdad?
Empleado:	Sí, señor.

Echando gasolina (putting in gas)

Lleno de super, por favor.	Fill it up with super (premium), please.
Dos mil pesetas, por favor.	2,000 pesetas of gas, please.
Cincuenta litros	50 liters
la gasolina	gas/gasoline
el gasóleo	diesel
la gasolina sin plomo	lead-free gasoline
super/normal	premium/regular
¿Quiere comprobar . . . ?	Please, could you check . . .?
el aceite/el agua/la presión	oil/water/tire pressure
Necesita medio litro	It needs half a liter
¿Cuánto le debo?	How much do I owe you?

Un pinchazo (a flat)

el taller	garage, body shop
¿Arregla usted pinchazos?	Do you fix flat tires?
¿Quiere reparar/arreglar . . . ?	Please repair/fix . . .
¿Puede cambiar . . . ?	Can you change . . . ?
el neumático	the tire
Tiene un agujero.	It has a hole.
¿Puede volver dentro de un rato?	Can you come back in a while?

Mi coche está averiado (my car has broken down)

(parts of the car are listed on p. 82)

No funciona el motor	The engine is not working
Mi coche no quiere arrancar	My car won't start
¿Dónde está el taller más cercano?	Where's the nearest garage?
¿Puede mandar un mecánico?	Can you send a mechanic?
¿Cuánto tiempo tardará?	How long will it take?
Puedo ponerlo en seguida	I can fit it at once
la marca/la matrícula	the make/the registration number

Road signs

Ceda el paso	Give way, yield
¡Cuidado!	Caution
Desviación	Detour
Dirección única	One-way street
Estacionamiento de automóviles	Parking
Estacionamiento prohibido	No parking
Obras	Roadwork (construction)
Paso prohibido	No entry
Peatones	Pedestrians
Peligro	Danger
Puesto de socorro	First aid station

**ESTACIONAMIENTO
PLAZA ESCANDALERA
SALIDA DE PEATONES**

**GARAJE LAVADO
ENGRASE
ACEITES–RUEDAS**

LAVADO 300 Pts

After an accident

Ha habido un accidente.	There has been an accident.
Hay gente herida.	Some people are hurt.
Llame la policía.	Call the police.
Llame una ambulancia/un médico.	Call an ambulance/a doctor.
¿Cuál es su numbre/su dirección?	What is your name/address?
su permiso de conducir	your driver's license
sus papeles de seguro	your insurance papers

OTHER USEFUL PHRASES

Ya está.	That's it.
Bueno, vamos a ver.	Well, let's have a look.
¿Cuánto le debo?	How much do I owe you?
Tengo un problema con . . .	I have a problem with . .

ILLNESS AND INJURY

Illness   In cases of minor injuries and illnesses, you may find the pharmacist very helpful. Pharmacists may sell and recommend medicine often only available by prescription in the U.S. If you take prescription medicine, always carry your prescription with you.

me duele la cabeza/I have a headache

Pilar doesn't feel well and goes to the doctor.

Médico: Hola, buenas tardes, siéntese por favor.
         Buenas tardes, doctor.
Pilar: Vamos a ver, ¿qué le pasa?
Médico: **No me siento bien. Me duele la**
Pilar: **cabeza,** no tengo apetito y me
         parece que **tengo fiebre.**
Médico: **¿Desde cuándo se siente así,**
         señora?
Pilar: Desde hace unos días . . . Y **me siento**
         mareada cuando me levanto por la
         mañana.
Médico: Por favor, **tiéndase aquí. Voy a**
         hacerle un examen. (Examines her)
         Por favor **abra la boca . . . Respire**
         profundo. . . . No se preocupe,
         señora, no es grave. **Tiene una gripe**
         y debe quedarse en cama. **Aquí tiene**
         una receta . . . Tome dos cucharadas
         cada tres horas. ¡Adiós, que se mejore
         pronto!
Pilar: Gracias y adiós.

En el consultorio (in the doctor's office)

Siéntese, por favor.	Sit down, please.
¿Qué le pasa?	What's wrong?
No me siento bien.	I don't feel well.
Me duele la cabeza/	I have a headache/
el estómago/la espalda	a stomachache/a backache
No tengo apetito.	I have no appetite.
Tengo fiebre.	I have a temperature (fever).
Me siento mareada	I feel dizzy
cuando me levanto	when I get up
¿Desde cuándo se siente así?	How long have you been feeling like this?
Desde hace unos días.	For a few days.
Tiéndase aquí.	Lie down here.
Voy a hacerle un examen.	I'm going to examine you.
Abra la boca.	Open your mouth.
Respire profundo.	Breathe deeply.
No se preocupe.	Don't worry.
No es grave.	It's not serious.
Tiene una gripe.	You have the flu.
Debe quedarse en cama.	You must stay in bed.
Aquí tiene una receta.	Here is a prescription.
Tome dos cucharadas	Take two tablespoonfuls
cada tres horas	every three hours
¡Que se mejore pronto!	Get better soon!

43

Things the doctor should know

Soy alérgico a . . .	I'm allergic to. . . .
. . . la penicilina	. . . penicillin
Soy diabético.	I'm diabetic.
Tomo la píldora.	I'm on the pill.
Estoy embarazada.	I'm pregnant.

Things that can happen to you

(Parts of the body are listed on p. 82.)

Me duele el . . ./la . . .	My . . . hurts
Me he roto . . ./Me he quemado . . .	I have broken . . ./I have burned . .
Me he torcido . . ./Me he cortado . . .	I have twisted . . ./I have cut . . .
Me ha picado un mosquito.	A mosquito has bitten me.
Tengo una insolación.	I have sunstroke.
Tengo diarrea	I have diarrhea
resfriado/catarro	a cold/flu
anginas/tos	a sore throat/cough
un moretón/una ampolla	a bruise/a blister
una quemadura/un salpullido	a burn/a rash
una picadura (de insecto)	a sting (insect)/bite
una intoxicación/una indigestión	food poisoning/indigestion
Tengo dolor de (estómago).	I have a (stomach) ache.
He tenido vómitos.	I've been vomiting.
Estoy estreñido.	I am constipated.
¿Necesito una receta?	Do I need a prescription?

Pharmacies These are identified by a green or red cross. Business hours are the same as other shops, but they are usually closed on Saturday afternoons. Each pharmacy remains open one night a week from 9 to 10 pm, and an emergency service is assured by a rotation system during holidays, at night and on weekends. Look for the on-duty sign **Farmacia de Guardia,** posted on pharmacy doors and printed in the local papers.

en la farmacia/at the pharmacy

Luisa has hay fever and goes to a pharmacy in Santander.

Luisa:	**¿Puede darme algo para la fiebre del heno, por favor?**
Druggist:	Sí señorita. (hands her a packet of pills) Tiene que tomar un comprimido cada cuatro horas. Son trescientas pesetas.
Luisa:	Muchas gracias, adiós.

At the pharmacy

(Pharmaceutical items and toiletries are listed on p. 81.)

¿Puede darme algo para . . .?	Can you give me something for . . .?
la fiebre del heno	hay fever
Tiene que tomar un comprimido/ la medicina	You must take a pill/tablet/ the medicine
cada cuatro horas/dos veces al día	every 4 hours/twice a day

the way it works

Making polite requests

Note:

¿**Quiere** comprobar el aceite?	Would you please check the oil?
¿**Quiere** arreglar el neumático	Would you please repair the tire?
¿**Puede** volver dentro de un rato?	Could you come back in a while?

Reflexive verbs

No **me** siento bien.	I don't feel well	(sentirse = to feel)
. . . cuando **me** levanto	. . . when I get up	(levantarse = to get up)

These are examples of verbs being used reflexively, indicating actions done by, to, or for oneself. The object of the verb is usually the same as the subject. Reflexive verbs are accompanied by a reflexive pronoun: **me** (myself), **te** (yourself), **se** (him/her/itself), **nos** (ourselves), **os** (yourselves), **se** (themselves):

Me llamo. . .	I am called . . .	from llamar**se** (to be called)
Te levantas	You get up	from levantar**se** (to get up)
Se abre	It opens	from abrir**se** (to open)
Nos bañamos	We bathe	from bañar**se** (to bathe)
Se sientan	They sit down	from sentar**se** (to sit down)

Note that the reflexive pronoun comes before the verb unless that verb is in the infinitive or imperative:

Siénte**se**   Sit down! (sentar**se**)   *but*   No **se** preocupe.   Don't worry.

I have a headache

Note that when talking about parts of your body you normally use "the" and not "a" or "my" as in English:

Me duele **la** cabeza.　I have a headache.
Abra **la** boca.　　　　Open your mouth.

How long ago . . .?

In Spanish use the phrase: **¿Desde cuándo?** + present tense.

¿Desde cuándo se siente así?　　How long have you been feeling this way?

and the reply

Desde hace unos días　Since a few days ago
Hace unos días　　　A few days ago

Hace (it makes) is part of **hacer** (to do or to make). Here is the present tense:

hago	I make	**hacemos**	we make
haces	you make	**hacéis**	you make
hace	he/she/it makes	**hace**	they make
	you make (formal)		you make (formal)

things to do

4.3　You are at a gas station. Tell the attendant in Spanish:

1 to fill up the tank　　　　**3** to check the oil
2 that you want 35 liters of premium　**4** to check the tire pressure

4.4　Your car has broken down and you are telephoning for help. You say:

1 that your car won't start　　**3** could they please send a mechanic?
2 that the ignition isn't working　**4** how long will that take?

4.5　You are not feeling well. Can you describe your symptoms to the doctor?

Doctor:　Buenos días, ¿qué le pasa?
You:　　[Say your stomach hurts and you have diarrhea]
Doctor:　¿Desde cuándo se siente así?
You:　　[For about a week]
Doctor:　Bueno, aquí tiene unos comprimidos para tomar tres
　　　　veces al día.
You:　　[Say thank you and goodbye]

4.6　In the pharmacy, you are looking for three items:

Phar.:　Buenos días, ¿puedo ayudarle?
You:　　[Ask if she can give you something for insect bites]
Pharm.:　Aquí tiene. ¿Algo más?
You:　　[Ask for some band-aids and some throat lozenges]

HOTELS AND CAMPSITES

Somewhere to stay   There are five official categories of Spanish **hotels,** ranging from the luxurious 5-star downwards. A 3-star hotel will usually offer you your own bathroom. In addition to the top-class hotels, there are **paradores,** state-run hotels which are often built in beautiful locations and sometimes situated in converted palaces and castles.

Less expensive forms of accommodation include **hostales** (small, often family-run, hotels) which are graded from 1 to 3 stars, **residencias** (economically priced hotels often without a restaurant), **pensiones** (boardinghouses often containing permanent residents), **albergues** (country inns), and **albergues de juventud** (youth hostels). The price of the room is written on a card on the back of the bedroom door, and does not vary according to the number of people in it. It does not always include breakfast. Prices of rooms throughout the range are generally cheaper than in the U.S. To book a hotel on the spot you can go to the local Tourist Office, but in the tourist season it is essential to make reservations in advance, particularly in the main tourist centers.

Looking for a hotel

¿Dónde hay un hotel?   Where is there a hotel?
¿Hay un hotel cerca de aquí?   Is there a hotel near here?
Busco un buen hotel   I'm looking for a good hotel
  en el centro de la ciudad   in the center of the city (downtown)

¿tiene una habitación doble?/do you have a double room?

As they are in the region of Ávila, Carmen and Tom decide to try their luck at a hotel recommended by Andrés Valbuena.

Recepcionista:	Buenos días, señores.
Carmen:	Buenos días. **¿Tiene una habitación doble, por favor?**
Recepcionista:	¿Para cuántas noches?
Carmen:	**Para dos noches.**
Recepcionista:	Bueno . . . ¿La quiere con baño, señora?
Carmen:	Sí, **con baño si es posible.**
Recepcionista:	Vamos a ver. (looks at list) Lo siento, señora. Tenemos habitaciones con lavabo pero no nos quedan con baño para hoy.
Carmen:	Bueno, no importa. **¿Cuánto es la habitación con lavabo?**
Recepcionista:	Son dos mil quinientas pesetas por noche.
Carmen:	**¿Está incluido el desayuno?**
Recepcionista:	Sí, todo incluido.
Carmen:	Está bien.

Reserving a room

Quisiera reservar una habitación	I'd like to reserve a room
para mañana/para miércoles	for tomorrow/for Wednesday
Lo siento. Está completo.	I'm sorry, the hotel's full.
¿Puede tener una habitación el jueves?	Would you have a room on Thursday?
He reservado una habitación.	I have reserved a room.
¿Hay habitaciones disponibles?	Are there any rooms available?
¿Tiene una habitación disponible?	Do you have a room available?
para esta noche	for tonight
para una noche	for one night
para dos/tres noches	for two/three nights
para una semana	for a week
para el miércoles	for Wednesday
para cuatro personas	for four people
Quiero una habitación doble	I want a double room
individual/sencilla	single
con baño/con ducha	with a bathroom/a shower
con lavabo	with a washbasin
con cama matrimonial/dos camas	with a double bed/twin beds
con un balcón/vista al mar	with a balcony/sea view
Tenemos habitaciones con ducha	We have rooms with a shower
No nos quedan . . .	We have no . . . left
¿Cuál es el precio?	What is the price?
¿Cuánto es por día?	How much is it per day?
la pensión completa/la media pensión	full board/half board
Es demasiado caro.	It is too expensive.
¿Tiene algo más barato?	Do you have anything cheaper?
¿Está incluido el desayuno?	Is breakfast included?
planta baja	ground floor
primer/segundo/tercer piso	first/second/third floor

he reservado una habitación/I have reserved a room

Andrés and his wife Asunción have reserved a room at the same hotel.

Andrés: Buenos días. **He reservado una
                habitación para dos noches.**
Recepcionista: ¿Cuál es su nombre, por favor?
Andrés: Andrés Valbuena.
Recepcionista: Ah, sí, . . . una habitación doble
                con baño. ¿Quiere llenar esta
                ficha, señor, y me deja su
                pasaporte?
Andrés: De acuerdo. (Fills in form)
Recepcionista: Firme aquí, por favor . . .
                Gracias. Su habitación es el
                número quince en el segundo
                piso. Aquí tiene su llave.
Andrés: Muchas gracias. **¿Se puede
                aparcar en la calle?**
Recepcionista: No, en esta calle no se puede,
                pero hay un aparcamiento
                detrás del hotel.

At the hotel

He reservado una habitación.	I have reserved a room.
¿Cuál es su nombre?	What is your name?
¿Quiere llenar esta ficha?	Please fill out this form.
Me deja su pasaporte	Let me have your passport
su carnet de identidad	your identity (I.D.) card
Es el número quince	It's number 15
en el segundo piso.	on the second floor.
Aquí tiene su llave.	Here is your key.
¿Puedo ver la habitación?	Can I see the room?
Esta habitación es demasiado pequeña.	This room is too small.
¿Me subirá el equipaje?	Will you have the luggage taken up?
¿Se puede aparcar en la calle?	Can you park in the street?
Hay un aparcamiento detrás del hotel.	There's a parking lot behind the hotel.

While you are there . . .

Me da la llave, por favor.	Please give me my key.
No funciona . . .	The . . . is not working
el agua caliente/fría	hot water/cold water
la luz/el interruptor de la luz	the light/the light switch
la radio/el televisor	the radio/the television set
¿A qué hora es el desayuno?/	What time is breakfast?/
la comida?/la cena?	lunch?/dinner?
¿Sirven el desayuno en la habitación?	Do you serve breakfast in the room?

Paying the bill

¿Me da la cuenta, por favor?	May I have the bill, please?
Creo que hay un error.	I think there is a mistake.
¿Puedo pagar con cheque?/tarjeta de crédito?	May I pay by check?/credit card?
¿Está incluido el servicio?	Is service included?

Camping If you want to camp, there are over 500 campsites to choose from, but it is advisable to reserve in advance for popular resorts in the high season. Camping I.D. cards are no longer required.

¿hay sitio?/is there a place?

Felipe, a student friend of Juan, has arrived with his tent at a campsite near Juan's house. He checks in at the office and talks to the guard.

Felipe:	Buenas tardes, señor. **¿Hay sitio?**
Guardián:	Sí, hay varios sitios. ¿Cuántas personas son?
Felipe:	**Somos tres. Tengo un coche y una tienda.**
Guardián:	¿Cuántas noches quieren pasar aquí?
Felipe:	**Dos noches, por favor.**
Guardián:	Puede ponerla allí. ¿Quiere llenar esta ficha, por favor?
Felipe:	De acuerdo. **¿Hay duchas calientes?**
Guardián:	Sí, pero no funciona el agua caliente en este momento.
Felipe:	Y, ¿hay electricidad?
Guardián:	Sí, ¿quieren toma de corriente?
Felipe:	Sí, por favor.

Prohibido acampar	No camping
¿Hay sitio?	Is there a place?
Hay varios sitios.	There are various places.
¿Cuántas personas son?	How many are you?
Somos dos.	We are two. (There are two of us.)
Tengo una tienda (de campaña)	I have a tent
una caravana	a van
Puede ponerla allí.	You can put it over there.
¿Quiere llenar esta ficha?	Please fill out this form.
¿Se puede comprar gas butano?	Can you buy butane gas?
¿Se puede alquilar un saco de dormir?	Can you rent a sleeping bag?
¿Dónde están las duchas calientes?/	Where are the hot showers?/
los cubos de basura?	the trash cans?
¿Dónde está el agua potable?	Where is the drinking water?
No funciona el agua.	The water isn't working.
los servicios/el retrete	toilets/lavatory
el agua/el grifo	water/tap
la piscina	swimming pool
¿Hay electricidad?	Is there electricity?
¿Quieren toma de corriente?	Do you want to plug in?
¿Se puede encender una hoguera?	Can you make a bonfire?

the way it works

The Present Perfect Tense

He reservado una habitación.   I have reserved a room.

This is an example of the present perfect tense, which is used in very much the same way as in English. It is formed with a part of the auxiliary verb **haber** (to have) + a past participle:

he reservado	I have reserved	**hemos** reservado	we have reserved
has reservado	you have reserved	**habéis** reservado	you have reserved
ha reservado	he/she has reserved	**han** reservado	they have reserved
	you have reserved		you have reserved

Note that the past participle **reservado** does not change its ending. Past participles are normally formed by taking the stem of the verb, e.g., **reserv-**, and adding on **-ado** (-ar verbs), or **-ido** (-er and -ir verbs).

things to do

5.1 Practice reserving different rooms at a hotel.

1

2

3

Quiero una habitación . . .

4

5

5.2 You arrive at a hotel after having reserved a room. Can you fill in your part of the conversation with the receptionist?

You: [Say good afternoon. You have reserved a room]
Recep.:   ¿Su nombre, por favor?
You: [Give your name]
Recep.:   A ver . . . Sí. Una habitación sencilla, número doce. ¿Quiere firmar aquí, por favor? . . . ¿Tiene equipaje?
You: [Say it's in the car]
Recep.:   El botones lo subirá. Aquí tiene su llave.
You: [Thank you very much]

5.3 You want to reserve a room for the night but you left it to the last minute.

You: [Ask if there is a room available]
Recep.:   Sí. ¿La quiere con baño?
You: [No, say you want a room with a washbasin]
Recep.:   Sólo tenemos una doble con baño.
You: [Ask how much the room is]
Recep.:   Tres mil seiscientas pesetas por noche.
You: [Say you are sorry but it's too expensive]

5.4 You are making inquiries about a campsite.

You: [Say good afternoon and ask if there is any room]
Guardián: Sí, hay varios sitios. ¿Cuántas personas son?
You: [Say you are four and that you have a van]
Guardián: ¿Cuánto tiempo quieren quedarse?
You: [A week]
Guardián: Bueno. Pueden poner la caravana cerca de la playa.

5.5 You are checking up on the facilities of a certain campsite. ¿Hay . . .?

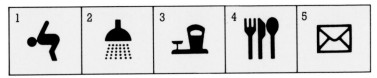

5.6 A lot of things don't seem to be working! Can you tell the guard?

1 the hot showers   **2** the toilets   **3** the electricity   **4** the tap (faucet)   **5** the drinking water

EATING OUT

Restaurants and mealtimes Spanish restaurants are officially classified by forks (**tenedores**); five forks is the most expensive, but you can often get a very good meal in a much more modest establishment. Look for the fixed-price menu (**menú del día**) which usually offers three courses and is often a very good value. Cheaper restaurants will often serve a one-dish meal (**plato combinado**), which combines several courses on one plate. Service is usually included (**servicio incluido**), but many people will leave a little extra for really good service.

en el restaurante/in the restaurant

Carmen and Tom have met up with Andrés and his wife Asunción and they have decided to eat out in a restaurant.

Tom:	**¿Hay una mesa libre?**
Camarero:	¿Es para cuántas personas, señor?
Tom:	**Somos cuatro.**
Camarero:	Pasen por aquí, señores. Tengo una mesa cerca de la ventana.

(They sit down at the table)

Camarero:	¿Qué van a comer, señores?
Asunción:	**Vamos a tomar el menú del día. De primero** quiero el gazpacho andaluz y **de segundo** la chuleta de ternera.
Carmen:	**Pues, para mí** los espárragos y el lomo de cerdo.
Andrés:	**Yo voy a tomar** la sopa de pescado y el bistec a la parrilla.
Camarero:	¿Cómo prefiere su bistec, señor?
Andrés:	**Lo prefiero poco hecho.**
Camarero:	(Turns to Tom) ¿Y usted, señor?
Tom:	**Pues a mí me gusta mucho** la paella. Voy a tomar la paella y una ensalada mixta.
Camarero:	Sí, señor. ¿Y para beber?
Tom:	**Tráiganos** una botella de Valdepeñas, y una botella de Chablis.
Carmen:	Y una botella de agua mineral, también.
Camarero:	En seguida, señores.

(Later the waiter asks them what they want for dessert)

Camarero:	¿Qué quieren **de postre**, señores?
Carmen:	Un flan con nata, un helado de vainilla y una tarta de manzana. **Y la cuenta, también, por favor.**

Ordering a meal

The table

¿**Puede recomendar un buen restaurante?**	Can you recommend a good restaurant?
Quiero reservar una mesa para las nueve.	I want to make a reservation for nine o'clock.
¿**Hay una mesa libre?**	Is there a table available?
¿**Para cuántas personas?**	For how many?
Somos cuatro.	There are four of us.
Una mesa para seis, por favor.	A table for six, please.
Pasen por aquí.	Come this way.
cerca de la ventana	near the window

The menu

¡**Oiga! ¡Camarero!**	Waiter!
Traiga el menú, por favor.	Bring the menu, please.
¿**Tiene un menú fijo?**	Do you have a set menu?
Vamos a tomar . . .	We'll have . . .
el menú del día	the menu of the day
el menú gastronómico	the gourmet menu
¿**Qué recomienda hoy?**	What do you recommend today?
¿**De qué consiste?**	What does it consist of?
De primero/de segundo	For the first course/second course
gazpacho andaluz	cold tomato soup
chuleta de ternera	veal cutlet
puntas de espárragos	asparagus tips
lomo de cerdo	pork loin
sopa de pescado	fish soup
bistec a la parrilla	grilled steak
bien hecho, regular, poco hecho	well done, medium, rare

paella valenciana	saffron rice and seafood (mussels, shrimp, etc.), with pieces of chicken, peas and peppers
ensalada mixta	tossed salad
¿Quiere algo de postre?	Would you like dessert?
No, gracias, no quiero nada.	No thank you, I don't want anything.
flan con nata	caramel custard with whipped cream
helado de vainilla	vanilla ice cream
tarta de manzana	apple tart

And to drink?

¿Y para beber?	What do you want to drink?
la lista de vinos	the wine list
Una botella de . . .	A bottle of . . . (See also Unit 1 p. 9.)
¿Tiene vino da la casa?	Do you have any house wine?
el agua mineral	mineral water
una coca-cola/una cerveza	a coke/a beer
café para todos	coffee for everyone

The check

La cuenta, por favor.	The check, please.

Meals   Breakfast (**el desayuno**) is a light meal consisting usually of coffee and bread or sweetrolls. Lunch (**el almuerzo, la comida**) is the main meal of the day and is eaten much later than in the U.S., between 2 and 3 pm, followed by a siesta. However, the tradition of a long late lunch is changing in the cities, where you will often find it is eaten earlier; the siesta is tending to disappear. The evening meal (**la cena**) is also eaten later—at 9 or 10 pm.

en el Hostal Lombraña/at the Hostal Lombraña

Juan meets his friend Felipe and together with Luisa and Miguel they go to a cheap restaurant in town. Juan is taking the orders.

Juan:	Amigos, ¿qué vais a tomar?
Luisa:	**Para mí, de primero,** sopa de fideos, por favor. Y después una tortilla de jamón con ensalada.
Juan:	¿Y tú, Miguel?
Miguel:	Pues, ¡yo tengo una hambre que me muero! **Voy a tomar** macarrones y albóndigas con salsa de tomate.
Juan:	Y ¿para ti, Felipe?
Felipe:	**Para mí un plato combinado.** Garbanzos y huevos con jamón.
Juan:	Y, ¿para beber?
Miguel:	Una coca-cola para mí, por favor.
Luisa:	Y para mí un zumo de naranja.

Para mí . . .	For me . . .
sopa de fideos	noodle soup
tortilla de jamón con ensalada	ham omelette and salad
(No) tengo hambre.	I am (not) hungry.
¡Tengo un hambre que me muero!	I am dying of hunger!
Voy a tomar macarrones.	I'll have macaroni.
albóndigas con salsa de tomate	meatballs in tomato sauce
garbanzos	chick-peas
huevos con jamón	ham and eggs
(No) tengo sed.	I am (not) thirsty.

Useful restaurant phrases

pan y cubierto	bread and cover charge
menú turístico	tourist menu
menú del día	menu of the day
platos combinados	combined dishes
postre a elegir	dessert choice
servicio incluido	service included
sal y pimienta	salt and pepper
Señoras	Ladies
Caballeros	Gentlemen
la mesa	table
la silla	chair
el cuchillo	knife
el tenedor	fork
la cuchara	spoon
el plato	plate, dish
aceite y vinagre	oil and vinegar

❊❊❊ MENÚ DEL DÍA ❊❊❊

gazpacho andaluz sopa de pescado puntas de espárragos ensalada mixta	paella valenciana huevos a la flamenca tortilla de jamón
chuleta de ternera lomo de cerdo bistec conejo al limón	flan con nata helado tarta de manzana fruta del tiempo queso

things to do

5.7 Look at this menu and decide what you and your two friends would like to eat: **De primero . . ., de segundo . . ., de postre . . .**

5.8 Things are not always easy when you try to order a meal . . .

Waiter:	¿Qué va a tomar, señor?
You:	[First, the mussels]
Waiter:	Lo siento, no tenemos hoy.
You:	[Well then, you'll have the fish soup]
Waiter:	Muy bien. ¿Y de segundo?
You:	[The codfish]
Waiter:	Lo siento, no queda . . .
You:	[Ask if he has fillet of sole]
Waiter:	Creo que sí, señor. ¿Y de postre?
You:	[An orange, please]
Waiter:	Sólo hay plátanos.
You:	[OK, you'll have a banana and could he bring the bill, please?]

SPORTS AND LEISURE

¿te gustan los deportes?/do you like sports?

Juan is talking to Miguel about sports.

Juan: **¿Qué deportes practicas** en Inglaterra?

Miguel: Pues, en invierno **juego al fútbol** y en verano al tenis. Pero soy muy malo para el tenis—**me gusta más** el fútbol.

Juan: **A mí me interesa la natación y la pesca,** sobre todo la pesca submarina.

Miguel: Y, **¿sabes hacer** esquí acuático?

Juan: Sí, **sé hacerlo pero prefiero la natación. Si te interesa** el fútbol, mañana hay un partido en el estadio. **¿Tienes ganas de** ir?

Miguel: ¡Oh sí! **Me gustaría mucho.** ¿Qué equipos juegan?

Juan: No sé, pero me parece que es un partido entre el Rácing y el Castellón.

Miguel: ¿A qué hora empieza?

Juan: **Empieza a las cinco de la tarde.** Bueno, hoy vamos a la taquilla para sacar las entradas.

RESULTADOS CUATRO ÚLTIMAS TEMPORADAS										PRÓXIMO BOLETO
En el descanso				Domingo 22 de noviembre	Al final del partido					(6 de diciembre)
83-84	84-85	85-86	86-87		83-84	84-85	85-86	86-87		
1-0	—	1-0	2-0	1 Barcelona-Cádiz.	4-1	—	1-0	2-0		1 Barcelona-Murcia
0-0	0-0	—	1-0	2 Murcia-Betis	1-0	0-1	—	3-0		2 Betis-Real Sociedad
—	—	1-0	—	3 Real Sociedad-Celta	—	—	1-1	—		3 Celta-Valladolid
—	—	—	—	4 Valladolid-Logroñés...	—	—	—	—		4 Logroñés-Real Madrid
1-0	—	—	0-0	5 Real Madrid-Mallorca	2-0	—	—	3-0		5 Mallorca-Spórting
—	—	—	1-0	6 Spórting-Sabadell	—	—	—	2-1		6 Sabadell-Zaragoza
0-1	1-1	0-0	0-0	7 Zaragoza-At. Madrid	2-2	1-1	0-0	1-0		7 At. Madrid-Osasuna
1-0	0-2	0-0	0-0	8 Osasuna-Athlétic	1-1	1-2	0-1	0-1		8 Athlétic-Las Palmas
0-1	0-0	1-1	0-0	9 Sevilla-Español	2-1	0-0	1-1	1-0		9 Valencia-Sevilla
0-1	—	—	—	10 Castellón-Rácing	1-1	—	—	—		10 Cádiz-Español
—	—	1-0	1-0	11 Sestao-Málaga	—	—	3-0	2-1		11 Rácing-Bilbao Ath.
0-0	—	1-1	0-0	12 Recreativo-Elche	1-0	—	2-1	0-1		12 Burgos-Sestao
—	—	—	0-0	13 Jerez-Oviedo	—	—	—	0-0		13 Málaga-Recreativo
0-0	3-2	1-1	0-0	14 Deportivo-Cartagena	3-0	4-2	2-1	1-0		14 Oviedo-Hércules

An interest in sports

(For a list of sports, see p. 83.)

¿Qué deportes practicas?	What sports do you play?
en invierno/en verano	in winter/in summer
juego al fútbol, tenis	I play soccer, tennis
el fútbol americano	football
Soy muy malo para . . .	I'm very bad at . . .
Me gusta más el fútbol.	I like soccer better.
No me gusta nada.	I don't like it at all.
A mí me interesa la natación/	I'm interested in swimming/
la pesca/la pesca submarina	fishing/deep-sea fishing
¿Sabes hacer el esquí acuático?	Do you know how to water-ski?
Sí, sé hacerlo.	Yes, I know how to.
Prefiero la natación.	I prefer swimming.
Si te interesa el fútbol	If you are interested in soccer
Hay un partido	There is a match (game)
en el estadio	in the stadium
¿Tienes ganas de ir?	Would you like to go?
Me gustaría mucho.	I'd love to.
¿Quiénes juegan?	Who is playing?
¿A qué hora empieza?	What time does it begin?
Empieza a las . . .	It begins at . . .
Vamos a la taquilla . . .	Let's go to the ticket office . . .
. . . para sacar las entradas	. . . to buy the tickets

Buying tickets

Dos entradas para el partido/	Two tickets for tomorrow's game or
la corrida de mañana	match/bullfight
de tribuna/de general	in the grandstand/on the terrace
	(general admission)
sol/sombra/sol y sombra	in the sun/shade/sun and shade

SIGHTSEEING

haciendo turismo/seeing places

Tom and Carmen are in Segovia where they visit the Oficina de Turismo.

Tom:	Buenas tardes. **Quisiera unos folletos sobre la región** y un plano de la ciudad, por favor.
Empleada:	Aquí tiene. ¿Algo más?
Tom:	**¿Tiene una lista de hoteles?**
Empleada:	Claro, señor.
Tom:	**¿Sabe a qué hora está abierto el Museo** del Alcázar?
Empleada:	Está abierto de nueve a doce y media por la mañana y de tres a siete por la tarde.
Tom:	Y, **¿cuánto vale la entrada?**
Empleada:	Trescientas cincuenta pesetas.
Tom:	Muchas gracias, señorita.

Quisiera unos folletos.	I'd like some brochures.
un plano de la ciudad	a map (plan) of the city
¿Tiene una lista de hoteles?	Do you have a list of hotels?
¿A qué hora está abierto . . .?	At what time is the . . . open?
¿A qué hora se abre?	At what time does it open?
¿A qué hora se cierra?	At what time does it close?
¿Cuánto vale la entrada?	How much does a ticket cost?
entrada gratuita	free entrance
abierto/cerrado	open/closed

Places to see

la catedral	cathedral	**el museo**	museum
el castillo, el alcázar	castle	**el palacio**	palace
la cueva	cave	**el ayuntamiento**	town hall
la iglesia	church	**el parque**	park
el claustro	cloister	**la plaza de toros**	bullring
la mezquita	mosque	**el monasterio**	monastery

the way it works

More verbs with vowel changes

We have already seen some verbs which have a change of vowel in the present tense (see Jueves, por la mañana, p. 38). We have also seen the following very commonly used verbs:

querer:	to want	⎫ e→ie	quiero	I want
tener:	to have	⎭	tienes	you have

This stem change occurs usually in the 1st, 2nd and 3rd persons singular and the 3rd person plural. In this unit we have:

empezar   *to begin:*   emp**ie**zo, emp**ie**zas, emp**ie**za, empezamos, empezáis, emp**ie**zan

cerrar   *to close:*   c**ie**rro, c**ie**rras, c**ie**rra, cerramos, cerráis, c**ie**rran

We also have a verb with a different vowel change:

jugar   *to play* u → **ue**: j**ue**go, j**ue**gas, j**ue**ga, jugamos, jugáis, j**ue**gan

What do you know?

¿**Sabes** (hacer el esquí acuático)?   Do you know how to (water-ski)?
Sé . . .   I know how to . . .
No **sé.**   I don't know.

To know something, or to know how to do something in Spanish is **saber.**

sé	I know	**sabemos**	we know
sabes	you know	**sabéis**	you know
sabe	he/she knows	**saben**	they know
	you know (formal)		you know (formal)

However, if you are talking about knowing a person or a place, you use the verb **conocer.**

No **conozco** la ciudad.   I don't know the city.
Encantado de **conocerle.**   Pleased to meet you.

Note that when talking about knowing a person, you insert **a** before that person.

Conocen a muchos americanos.   They know many Americans.

Here is the present tense:

conozco	I know	**conocemos**	we know
conoces	you know	**conocéis**	you know
conoce	he/she knows	**conocen**	they know
	you know (formal)		you know (formal)

Question words

Here is a list of some of the question words from the dialogues in this unit and elsewhere:

¿**Qué?**	What?	¿**Qué** deportes practicas?
¿**Quién?**/¿**Quiénes?**	Who?	¿**Quiénes** juegan?
¿**Cuándo?**	When?	¿**Cuándo** empieza?
¿**Cuánto?**	How much?	¿**Cuánto** vale la entrada?
¿**Cuántos/as?**	How many?	¿**Cuántas** personas son?
¿**Cuál?**	Which?	¿**Cuál** es su nombre?
¿**Cómo?**	How?	¿**Cómo** te llamas? (literally, How are you called?)
		¿**Cómo** es? (literally, How is it?)

Note that question words always carry a written accent.

things to do

You are being asked what sports you play.

Interviewer: ¿Qué deportes practicas?
You: [Say you play tennis and you like swimming]
Interviewer: ¿Te gusta también el fútbol?
You: [Say you don't like it at all]
Interviewer: ¿Sabes jugar al golf?
You: [Yes, you know how to but you prefer tennis]

¿Te gusta el deporte? Me gusta.../No me gusta.../Soy muy malo para...

1 Luisa likes ball games but hates water sports. When asked what sports she likes, what does she say?
2 Juan likes most things to do with water, but is no good at ball games. When asked which sports he likes, what does he say?
3 Now can you say what sports or games you like, what you don't like, and what you are bad at?

Felipe takes Luisa to see the Tito Bustillo cave, where they talk to the **empleada**, the cashier.

Felipe: [Two tickets, please]
Empleada: [Say how much two cost]
Felipe: [Ask what time they open]
Empleada: [Say they open at 3 pm]
He also takes her to the Claustro Romano.
Felipe: [Two tickets, please]
Empleada: [Say how much two cost]
Felipe: [Ask what time it closes]
Empleada: [Say it closes at 7 pm]

Can you match the following questions and answers?

1 ¿Te gusta la equitación?   **(a)** Sí, sé hacerlo.
2 ¿Qué equipo juega?   **(b)** Prefiero la pesca.
3 ¿Prefieres la pesca o la natación?   **(c)** De nueve a doce.
4 ¿Sabes jugar al ajedrez (chess)?   **(d)** No, no me gusta nada.
5 ¿A qué hora está abierta?   **(e)** Juega el equipo de
                                                    Salamanca.

You are introduced to señor Santillana at a party (**una reunión**) and strike up a conversation with him. Can you ask these questions in Spanish?

1 Ask him if he knows Victor, a colleague from your office in Dallas.
    ¿Conoces a Víctor, un colega de mi oficina en Dallas?
2 Ask if he knows Conchita, a friend of your wife.
3 Does he know how to play chess?
4 Ask him if he knows when the party finishes. (use *se termina*)
5 Say you know your wife would like to meet him.

VACATION PLANS

las vacaciones/vacations

Carmen is interviewing various students about the sort of vacations they like.

Carmen:	¿Cuándo piensas ir de vacaciones este año?
Estudiante:	Pues, **pienso ir a principios de septiembre.**
Carmen:	Y, ¿adónde piensas ir? ¿Al extranjero, a las montañas, al mar?
Estudiante:	Este **año voy a Cantabria**—primero a Santander.
Carmen:	Y, ¿qué vas a hacer allí?
Estudiante:	Voy a alquilar un coche y **visitaré muchos sitios.** Tengo ganas de ver los Picos de Europa.
Carmen:	Y, ¿cuánto tiempo te quedarás en Asturias?
Estudiante:	**Me quedaré unos quince días,** o sea, **volveré a mi casa** dentro de tres semanas, nada más. Estoy estudiando idiomas y vuelvo a clase el 21 de septiembre.

Vacations

¿Cuándo piensas ir . . .?	When do you think you'll go . . .?
. . . de vacaciones?	. . . on vacation?
Pienso ir	I'm thinking of going
a principios de	at the beginning of
a fines de	at the end of
septiembre	September (for months see p. 79)
¿Adónde piensas ir?	Where are you thinking of going?
al extranjero	abroad
a las montañas/al mar	to the mountains/to the sea
al campo	to the countryside
Voy a alquilar un coche.	I'm going to rent a car.

SÁBADO   SATURDAY

Visitaré muchos sitios.	I will visit many places.
Tengo ganas de ver . . .	I feel like seeing . . .
los Picos de Europa	the Asturian mountains
¿Cuánto tiempo te quedarás?	How long will you stay?
Me quedaré unos quince días.	I'll stay about two weeks (a fortnight).
Volveré dentro de tres semanas.	I'll return within three weeks.
Volveremos a casa.	We'll return home.
Estoy estudiando idiomas.	I'm studying languages.
vuelvo a clase	I go back to class

Dates

¿En qué fecha estamos?	What's the date today?
el primero de mayo	May 1
el cuatro de abril	April 4
el veintiuno de septiembre	September 21
sábado, diez de octubre	Saturday, October 10
el mes pasado	last month
la semana próxima	next week
este año	this year
el cumpleaños	birthday
Navidad/Pascua	Christmas/Easter
ayer/hoy/mañana	yesterday/today/tomorrow
todos los días	every day
(días) laborables	work days
(días) festivos	public holidays, feast days

ENTERTAINMENT

Going to the movies   In the city, movie theaters generally have three showings: one at about 4:30 pm, the next at about 7:30 pm, and the last at about 10 or 11 pm. You may find a continuous session (**sesión continua**) starting at about 4 or 5 pm. In the country, there may only be two sessions (**función de la tarde** and **función de la noche**). Many foreign films are shown and most are dubbed into Spanish. When they are shown in the original language with subtitles, this is indicated by **V.O.** (**versión original**). It is customary to tip the usher (**acomodador/a**).

> ## SESIÓN CONTINUA
>
> **Cristal.** (2) / ☎ 234 93 53 / Bravo Murillo, 120; Cuatro Caminos / *Metro* Cuatro Caminos.
> —**Luna de lobos** y **Superedetective en Hollywood II.** No recomendadas para menores de 13 años. Continua desde las 4.35 de la tarde.
> **España.** (3) / ☎ 269 56 70 / General Ricardos, 4 / *Metro* Marqués de Vadillo. Autobús 34.
> —**Cuenta conmigo** y **Nadine.** Toleradas. 4.30.
> **Esproceda.** (4) / ☎ 441 92 51 / Alonso Cano, 28; Chamberí / *Metro* Ríos Rosas.
> —**Las nuevas aventuras de Popeye** y **Superman IV.** Laborables, continua, 5; sábados y festivos. 4.30. Toleradas.
> **Europa.** (3) / ☎ 233 10 48 / Bravo Murillo, 160; Tetuán / *Metro* Estrecho.

¿qué te gustaría hacer?/what would you like to do?

Felipe invites Luisa to go out with him but they don't know where to go . . .

Felipe:	¿Qué vamos a hacer esta noche?
Luisa:	Pues, no sé. **¿Te gustaría ir a una discoteca?**
Felipe:	No, bailar no me gusta nada.
Luisa:	Entonces, **¿qué te gusta hacer en tu tiempo libre?**
Felipe:	**Me gusta ir al cine,** me gusta salir con amigos, me gusta escuchar música. Y tú, **¿cuáles son tus aficiones?**
Luisa:	Es difícil. Me gusta bailar, me gusta mucho ir al teatro y también me gusta escuchar música. **Me encanta la música pop.**
Felipe:	Ésa no me gusta. **Prefiero la música clásica.** Toco el piano y estoy aprendiendo la flauta.
Luisa:	Pues, mira. **¿por qué no vamos al cine?**
Felipe:	Buena idea. ¿Sabes qué películas ponen en este momento?
Luisa:	No. Hay que mirar la cartelera.

Going out or staying in?

¿Qué te gusta hacer?	What do you like doing?
¿Qué vamos a hacer?	What shall we do?
¿Te gustaría ir a . . .?	Would you like to go to . . .?
¿Qué te parece ir a . . .?	What do you think of going to . . .?
No puedo salir esta tarde.	I can't go out this evening.
Buena idea.	Good idea.
Me gustaría mucho.	I would like to very much.
Me encantaría.	I would love to.
No tengo ganas.	I don't feel like it.
Bailar no me gusta nada.	I don't like dancing at all.
tu tiempo libre	your free time
Me gusta . . .	I like . . .
ir al cine/al teatro	going to the movies/theater
salir con amigos	going out with friends
ir a los toros	going to a bullfight
escuchar música	listening to music
bailar	dancing
pasear/dar paseos	going for walks
ver la televisión	watching television
leer	reading
¿Cuáles son tus aficiones?	What are your hobbies?
Es difícil.	It's difficult.

Listening to or playing music

Me encanta . . .	I adore . . .
la música pop	pop music

la música clásica	classical music
ir a un concierto	going to a concert
la orquesta/el cantante	orchestra/singer
Toco el piano/la flauta/el violín/	I play the piano/flute/violin/
el clarinete/la trompeta/la guitarra	the clarinet/trumpet/guitar
Estoy aprendiendo	I am learning

Going to the movies

¿Por qué no vamos al cine?	Why don't we go to the movies?
una película	film
¿Sabes qué películas ponen?	Do you know what films are showing?
en este momento	at the moment
V.O. subtitulada	original version with subtitles
sesión continua	continuous performance
Autorizada para todos los públicos	Suitable for everyone
No recomendada para menores de	Not recommended for under 18
18 años	
Hay que mirar la cartelera	We'll have to look in the entertainment page

Buying a ticket for a show

la taquilla	box office
asientos limitados	limited seating
la butaca/el anfiteatro	box seats/balcony
¿Hay localidades para esta función?	Are there seats for this performance?
Localidades desde 250 pesetas	Seats from 250 pesetas
Dos entradas, por favor.	Two tickets, please.
¿A qué hora empieza el espectáculo?	What time does the show start?
¿Hay descuentos para estudiantes?	Are there student discounts?
la localidad, la entrada	ticket
venta anticipada	tickets in advance

the way it works

I'm learning the flute

Estoy estudiando	I am studying
Estoy aprendiendo	I am learning

It's useful to be able to use the continuous present tense which is formed in a similar way to the English "I am . . . ing."
Use the present tense of **estar + present participle**, which is formed by taking the stem of the verb:

escuch- and adding **-ando**	for -ar verbs
aprend- and adding **-iendo**	for -er and -ir verbs

The future tense

Visitaré muchos sitios.	I will visit many places.
Me quedaré quince días.	I will stay two weeks.
Volveré a mi casa.	I'll return home.

These are examples of the future tense which is used as an alternative to **ir a +** infinitive: **Voy a** alquilar un coche.   I'm going to rent a car.

The future tense is formed normally by taking the infinitive and adding the following endings:

visitar-**é**	I will visit	visitar-**emos**	we will visit
visitar-**ás**	you will visit	visitar-**éis**	you will visit
visitar-**á**	he/she will visit	visitar-**án**	they will visit
	you will visit (formal)		you will visit (formal)

These endings are the same for all verbs but some verbs form the future stem from a variation of the infinitive. Some common examples are:

salir:	to go out	sal**dré**	I will go out
tener:	to have	ten**dré**	I will have
hay:	there is	ha**brá**	there will be

things to do

6.6 **¿Cuáles son tus aficiones?** What do you like doing in your spare time?

Me encanta   me gusta mucho   me gusta   no me gusta nada

En casa	*Por la tarde*	*De vacaciones*
1 ver la televisión	salir con amigos	ir a las montañas
2 jugar a las cartas	ir al cine	ir a la playa
3 leer	ir al teatro	visitar muchos sitios
4 escuchar la música	ir a un restaurante	hacer el esquí
5 cocinar (to cook)	ir a una discoteca	ir al extranjero

6.7
1 What is being advertised here?
2 What does the ad say about César Delgado and Teresa del Sol?
3 What days of the week is it open?
4 What times of day?
5 Where is the exhibition held?

> **GALERÍAS DE ARTE**
> **EXPOSICIONES**
> **Ateneo de Madrid.** Sala de exposiciones Santa Catalina / Santa Catalina, 10.
> —Exposición de **César Delgado**, pintor, y **Teresa del Sol**, ceramista. De lunes a sábados, de 18 a 20 horas.

la exposición	exhibition
la ceramista	ceramic artist

6.8 You want to buy tickets for a theater performance.

1 Ask if there are any tickets for tonight.
2 Ask the price of the tickets.
3 Say you would like two tickets.
4 Ask how much it comes to.
5 Ask what time the show starts.

USING THE TELEPHONE

You can find public phones in individual booths (**cabinas**), telephone offices (**locutorios**), and many bars and restaurants. Some phones take Euro coins and others take special phone cards (**tarjetas telefónicas**), which can be purchased at a tobacco shop (**estanco**) or newsstand (**quiosco**). International calls made from a hotel can be subject to a large surcharge, so take advantage of phone offices or cards to save money.

una llamada telefónica/a telephone call

Luisa suggests it might be a good idea to telephone Pilar to let her know when they are returning to Madrid.

Luisa:	¿Oye, Juan, vas a llamar a tu madre?
Juan:	Sí, sí, la llamaré ahora misma.
Luisa:	**¿Cuál es tu número?** Voy a marcarlo si quieres.
Juan:	Es el 33-78-92.
Luisa:	(dials the number) Aquí tienes. (Juan takes over)
Pilar:	**Diga.**
Juan:	**Hola, mamá. Soy yo,** Juan. ¿Qué tal?
Pilar:	Hola. ¿Qué hay? ¿Qué tal Luisa y Miguel? ¿Qué estáis haciendo? ¿Cuándo vais a volver a Madrid?

Juan: Pues, estamos muy bien . . . Llegamos el miércoles por la tarde, . . . el jueves Luisa y Miguel se dieron una vuelta por Santander y compraron unas cosas. . . . El sábado yo fui con Miguel a un partido de fútbol y Luisa fue en coche con un amigo mío a . . . algún sitio. ¿Adónde fuiste, Luisa?

Luisa: A muchos sitios—a Cangas de Onís y . . .

Juan: (to Pilar) Fueron a Cangas de Onís. Y por la noche se fueron al cine. En fin, lo estamos pasando muy bien.

Pilar: ¿Con quién salió Luisa? ¿Con Martín?

Juan: No . . . con Felipe. Es un buen chico, sabes, muy serio.

Pilar: ¡Ah, sí! Me acuerdo . . . Bueno, y ¿cuándo pensáis volver?

Juan: A lo mejor, mañana. Cogeremos el tren de las once y media y llegaremos a eso de las seis de la tarde.

Pilar: Muy bien. Entonces, hasta mañana.

Juan: **Adiós, mamá.**

Telephone talk

llamar por teléfono	to telephone
¿Cuál es tu/su número?	What's your number?
Mi número de teléfono es . . .	My telephone number is . . .
Quiero hablar con . . .	I want to speak to . . .
marcar	to dial
Diga, Dígame	Hello (when picking up receiver)
¿Quién habla?	Who's speaking?
¿De parte de quién?	Who's calling?
Llamo de parte de . . .	I'm calling for . . .
Soy . . .	It's . . . (+ speaker's name)
Hable más despacio/lento.	Speak more slowly.
No entiendo.	I don't understand.
¿Quiere dejarle algún recado?	Do you want to leave him a message?
¿Quiere decirle que . . .?	Please tell him that . . .
la guía telefónica	telephone directory
el teléfono internacional	international telephone
el prefijo	area code
el cobro revertido	reverse charge (collect) call

Saying what you did

Llegamos el miércoles.	We arrived on Wednesday.
dieron una vuelta por Santander	they walked around Santander
compraron unas cosas	they bought some things
Yo fui a un partido de fútbol.	I went to a soccer match.

Carmen fue en coche a . . .	Carmen drove to . . .
algún sitio	some place
¿Adónde fuisteis?	Where did you go?
Fuimos a Cangas de Onís.	We went to Cangas de Onís.
se fueron al cine	they went to the movies
¿Con quién salió Luisa?	Who did Luisa go out with?
Un buen chico, muy serio	A good young man, very serious
Sí, me acuerdo	Yes, I remember

the way it works

Saying what you are doing

¿Qué estáis haciendo?	What are you doing?
Lo estamos pasando muy bien.	We are having a good time.

Saying what you intend to do

Le llamaré ahora mismo.	I'll call her at once.
¿Cuándo pensáis volver?	When do you intend to come back?
A lo mejor, mañana.	Probably tomorrow.
Cogeremos el tren.	We'll catch the train.
Llegaremos a eso de las seis.	We'll arrive about six.

Saying what happened

Fui a un partido de fútbol.	I went to a soccer match.
¿Adónde fuiste?	Where did you go?

llegamos (we arrived), pasearon (they walked around), compraron (they bought), salió (she went out).

All these verbs are in the **preterite** tense, which is used a great deal in Spanish for relating past events. The endings for this tense are as follows:

-ar verbs, e.g., **comprar** (to buy)

compré	I bought	compramos	we bought
compraste	you bought (fam.)	comprasteis	you bought (fam.)
compró	he/she/you bought	compraron	they/you bought

-er verbs, e.g., **volver** (to return)

volví	I returned	volvimos	we returned
volviste	you returned (fam.)	volvisteis	you returned (fam.)
volvió	he/she/you returned	volvieron	they/you returned

-ir verbs, e.g., **salir** (to leave)

salí	I left	salimos	we left
saliste	you left (fam.)	salistesi	you left (fam.)
salió	he/she/you left	salieron	they/you left

A number of verbs are irregular in the preterite. Here are three common ones:

dar (to give)

di	I gave	**dimos**	we gave
diste	you gave	**disteis**	you gave
dio	he/she gave, you gave	**dieron**	they gave, you gave

ir (to go) and **ser** (to be) (**ir** and **ser** share the same pattern)

fui	I went	**fuimos**	we went
fuiste	you went	**fuisteis**	you went
fue	he/she went, you went	**fueron**	they went, you went

hacer (to do, make)

hice	I made	**hicimos**	we made
hiciste	you made	**hicisteis**	you made
hizo	he/she/it made, you made	**hicieron**	they made, you made

Some verbs have a change in the spelling to enable them to keep the same stem sound throughout: **llegar** (to arrive), **llegué** (I arrived).

things to do

7.1 You are being interviewed about your daily routine.

Interviewer: ¿A qué hora se levanta?
You: (I get up at 7:30)
Interviewer: ¿Y qué hace después?
You: (I have my breakfast) (use **desayunarse**)
Interviewer: ¿A qué hora sale de la casa?
You: (I leave at 9:00 and catch the bus to my office)
Interviewer: ¿Vuelve a casa para almorzar? (to have lunch)
You: (Yes, I come home at noon and have lunch. Then I do my shopping [**voy de compras**] and go back to the office in the afternoon)

7.2 The interviewer now wants to know what you did last Tuesday. Use the phrases from the previous exercise and put the verbs into the past tense:

Interviewer: El martes, ¿a qué hora se levantó? You: . . . .
Interviewer: Y ¿qué hizo después? You: . . . .
Interviewer: ¿A qué hora salió de la casa? You: . . . .
Interviewer: ¿Volvió a casa para almorzar? You: . . . .
Interviewer: ¿Qué hizo después? You: . . . .

7.3 Using the telephone. The telephone rings and you pick up the receiver. Can you take your part in a telephone conversation in which arrangements are being made?

You: [Hello]
Juan: Hola, soy Juan. ¿Qué hay? Oye, quisiera invitarte a cenar esta tarde. Hoy es nuestra última noche en Santander, y mañana volvemos a Madrid.
You: [Say you'd like to very much. Ask what time to come]
Juan: Pues, a eso de las ocho. ¿Sabes dónde estamos?
You: [Say yes, you know where he lives and you'll take a taxi]
Juan: Bueno, entonces, hasta pronto.

DESCRIBING THINGS & PEOPLE

¿puede decirme cómo eran?/can you tell me what were they like?

Carmen has been asked to give a description of a couple she saw shoplifting.

Policía:	**¿Cómo eran,** por favor?
Carmen:	Pues, mire, **había un chico y una chica.** El chico tenía unos veinte años, y la chica quizás veinticinco.
Policía:	**¿La chica era rubia o morena?**
Carmen:	**Era rubia y bastante baja. Tenía los ojos azules** y el pelo largo y rubio.
Policía:	Y, ¿qué llevaba?
Carmen:	Llevaba una falda negra muy corta, y un jersey verde.
Policía:	¿Y el chico?
Carmen:	Era muy alto y moreno. **Llevaba vaqueros y botas** y una chaqueta de cuero.
Policía:	Muy bien. ¿Y a qué distancia de ellos estaba usted?
Carmen:	Estaba a unos tres metros, nada más.
Policía:	¿Qué estaban haciendo?
Carmen:	Metían unos objetos en un bolso y de repente me vieron. Al verme se escaparon sin esperarse.

Describing what you saw

¿Cómo eran?	What did they look like?
Había un chico y una chica.	There were a boy and a girl.
tenía unos veinte años	he was about 20
tenía quizás veinticinco	she perhaps 25
¿Era rubia o morena?	Was she blonde or brunette?
bastante baja	quite short
tenía los ojos azules/castaños	she had blue/brown eyes
el pelo largo	long hair
¿Qué llevaba?	What was she wearing?
alto y moreno	tall and dark
llevaba vaqueros	he was wearing jeans
¿A qué distancia de ellos estaba?	What distance away were you?
estaba a unos tres metros	I was about 3 meters away
Metían unos objetos	They were putting some things
en un bolso . . .	in a bag . . .
de repente me vieron	they suddenly caught sight of me
Al verme se escaparon	As soon as they saw me they fled
sin esperarse	in a flash (literally, "without waiting")

SAYING GOODBYE

hasta el año que viene/see you next year

Juan's party is in full swing and all the guests are enjoying themselves.
They are out in the garden after supper.

Luisa: ¡Qué noche más estupenda! Lo hemos pasado muy bien aquí en España.

Felipe: **Siento mucho que no puedas quedarte en Santander.** Pero volverás el año próximo, ¿me prometes?

Luisa: Seguramente.

Felipe: ¿Qué cosas te gustan más en España?

Luisa: Pues, no hay problema. Hace buen tiempo todos los días, la gente es muy simpática, y **todo el mundo se divierte** mucho.

Felipe: Sí, es verdad. Pero, ¿qué pasa? **¡Está lloviendo!** Y el pronóstico para mañana es malo—habrá tormentas. Eso no puede ser . . .

(They go inside, where Juan is being a good host.)

Juan: Hola, Felipe. ¿Quieres otra bebida?

Felipe: No, gracias, ya es tarde y tengo que irme. Oye, Juan, ¿por qué no vamos a Inglaterra en la primavera?

Juan: Me gustaría mucho. Estarás en Madrid la semana próxima, ¿verdad?

Felipe: Claro que sí. Bueno, pues te veré en Madrid. Muchas gracias y adiós a todos.

Juan: Adiós, hasta luego.

Party conversation

¡Qué noche más estupenda!	What a lovely evening!
Lo hemos pasado muy bien.	We have really enjoyed ourselves.
Siento mucho que no puedas quedarte.	I'm sorry you can't stay.
Volverás el año próximo,	You'll come back next year,
¿me prometes?	you promise me?
seguramente/no hay problema	certainly/no problem
Hace buen tiempo	It's good weather
todos los días	every day
la gente es muy simpática	people are nice
todo el mundo se divierte	everyone enjoys himself
Sí, es verdad.	Yes, it's true.
¿Qué pasa?	What's happening?
Está lloviendo.	It's raining.
El pronóstico para mañana . . .	The forecast for tomorrow . . .
habrá tormentas	there will be thunderstorms
¡Eso no puede ser!	That's not possible!

¿Quieres otra bebida?	Do you want another drink?
Tengo que irme.	I have to go.
¿Por qué no vamos a Inglaterra?	Why don't we go to England?
en la primavera	in the spring
Te veré en Madrid, ¿verdad?	I'll see you in Madrid, won't I?
Claro que sí.	Certainly.
Muchas gracias y adiós.	Many thanks and goodbye.
Adiós, hasta luego.	Goodbye, till then.
Hasta el año que viene.	See you next year.

The weather (El tiempo)

¿Qué tiempo hace?	What's the weather like?
Hace sol./Habrá sol.	It's sunny./There will be sunshine.
Hace frío/viento.	It's cold/windy.
Hace buen/mal tiempo.	It's good weather/bad weather.
Está nublado.	It's cloudy.
Está lloviendo/nevando.	It's raining/snowing.
Habrá temporal/tormenta.	There will be a gale/storm.
el cielo nuboso/cubierto	cloudy/overcast sky
el cielo despejado	clear sky
la lluvia/el chubasco	rain/shower
la nieve/el granizo/la niebla	snow/hail/fog

the way it works

Saying what someone was like

Tenía unos veinte años.	He was about 20.
Era rubia y bastante baja.	She was blonde and quite short.
Estaba a unos tres metros.	I was about 3 meters away.

These are examples of the **imperfect** tense. This tense is mainly used for past descriptions of people and places, for saying what you or someone else was doing, or what was happening. It is usually formed by taking the stem of the verb and adding on endings as follows:

-ar verbs e.g., **llevar** (to wear, carry)

llev-**aba**	I was wearing	llev-**ábamos**	we were wearing
llev-**abas**	you were wearing	llev-**abais**	you were wearing
llev-**aba**	he/she was wearing you were wearing	llev-**aban**	they were wearing you were wearing

-er and **-ir** verbs share the same endings:

ten-**ía**	I had	ten-**íamos**	we had
ten-**ías**	you had	ten-**íais**	you had
ten-**ía**	he/she had, you had	ten-**ían**	they had, you had

A handful of verbs form the imperfect differently, among them **ser** (to be).

era	I was	**éramos**	we were
eras	you were	**erais**	you were
era	he/she was, you were	**eran**	they were, you were

The imperfect is often used in conjunction with the preterite when two things are happening at the same time: **Metían** unos objetos en un bolso cuando me **vieron**. (They were putting some things in a bag when they saw me.)

Al verme . . .

Al verme se escaparon.　　On seeing me, they escaped (ran away).

The use of **al + infinitive** is very common to join two verbs with the same subject: **Al acabar** sus estudios volvió a Madrid. (On finishing her studies, she returned to Madrid.)

The weather is terrific!

Hace muy buen tiempo.　　It's lovely weather.

Hace comes from **hacer** (to make) and is often used when talking about the weather. (See p. 46 for present-tense forms.)

It's sunny every day!

todos los días　　every day　　**todo el** mundo　　everyone

To say "all" or "every" use **todo, toda, todos, todas.**

Really and truly

verdaderamente really　**seguramente** surely　**súbitamente** suddenly

To form an adverb you normally add **-mente** on to the feminine form of the adjective. Other common adverbs include:

desgraciadamente unluckily　**afortunadamente** fortunately

things to do

7.4 What were you doing in Madrid? Some time ago you were living there and you are now being interviewed about it.

Interviewer:	¿Qué hacías en Madrid?
You:	[Say you were studying Spanish]
Interviewer:	¿Dónde vivías?
You:	[Say you were living in the calle de Serrano with a family]
Interviewer:	¿Había unos hijos en la familia?
You:	[Yes, there was a daughter]
Interviewer:	¿Cómo se llamaba la hija y cuántos años tenía?
You:	[She was called Mari-Carmen and she was 23]

Interviewer:	¿Qué hacías por la tarde?
You:	[You went out with friends, or sometimes you stayed at home and read, or watched television]
Interviewer:	En fin, ¿te gustaba Madrid?
You:	[Say yes, you liked it very much and you had a wonderful time]

5 Miguel thinks he has lost his watch and he goes to the police station to report it. Look at the following interview and see if you can understand it:

Miguel:	Buenas tardes. Creo que he perdido mi reloj en la calle.
Policía:	¿Cuándo lo perdió, señor?
Miguel:	Pues, esta tarde fui al partido de fútbol y estoy seguro de que lo llevaba cuando salí del estadio.
Policía:	Sí, señor, pero ¿cuándo se dio usted cuenta de que lo había perdido?
Miguel:	Al llegar a mi casa me di cuenta de que no lo tenía. Lo busqué por todas partes pero no lo encontré.
Policía:	¿El reloj era de gran valor, señor?
Miguel:	Pues, no sé exactamente, pero mi abuela me lo dio como regalo.
Policía:	Bueno, . . . ¿Quiere llenar este formulario, por favor, con todos los detalles, y veremos? . . . ¿Vive aquí en Santander?
Miguel:	No, mañana vuelvo a Madrid.

The language of losing something

perder	to lose	**He perdido**	I have lost
robar	to steal	**Me han robado**	Someone has stolen
buscar	to look for	**Busqué**	I looked
encontrar	to find	**No encontré**	I didn't find
darse cuenta	to realize	**Me di cuenta**	I realized
el reloj	watch	**la cartera**	wallet
la bolsa	purse	**la cámara**	camera

Now try to report what Miguel said, with the help of the following phrases:
Esta tarde, Miguel . . . a un partido de fútbol y . . . seguro de que lo . . .
cuando . . . del estadio. Al llegar a su casa . . . cuenta de que no lo . . .
Lo . . . por todas partes pero no lo . . .

7.6 **El pronóstico para mañana** (The forecast for tomorrow—showing that the weather in Spain isn't always perfect!)

Cantábrico. Cielo muy nuboso o cubierto con chubascos, que serán en forma de nieve en altitudes superiores a los 1.000 metros. Los vientos serán fuertes del noroeste. Habrá temporal fuerte con mar arbolada en la zona marítima. Máximas de 6°C y mínimas de −5°C.

1 Will the sky be clear or cloudy?
2 Will there be rain or snow showers?
3 What direction will the winds be from?
4 Where will there be a gale?
5 What will be the minimum temperature?

7.7 **¿Qué tiempo hace?** Here is a weather map of Spain. Can you say what the weather is like:

1 en el mar mediterráneo?
2 en los Pirineos?
3 en Madrid?
4 en el sur de España?
5 en el noroeste?

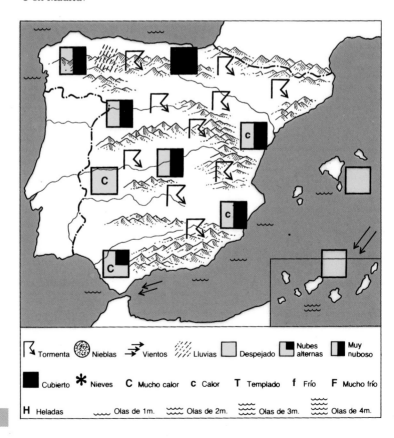

Tormenta   Nieblas   Vientos   Lluvias   Despejado   Nubes alternas   Muy nuboso

Cubierto   Nieves   **C** Mucho calor   **c** Calor   **T** Templado   **f** Frío   **F** Mucho frío

H Heladas   Olas de 1m.   Olas de 2m.   Olas de 3m.   Olas de 4m.

1.1 1 Buenos días, señora. ¿Cómo está usted? 2 Buenas tardes, señor. ¿Cómo está? 3 Hola, ¿cómo estás?/Muy bien, gracias. 4 Hola, buenas tardes, ¿qué tal?
1.2 Sí, soy Annie Rogers./Sí, éste es mi hermano, Felipe./Sí, es mi maleta./Sí, es su maleta.
1.3 1 ¿Es usted la señora Barillo? 2 ¿Es ésta su maleta? 3 ¿Dónde está? 4 ¿Cómo está usted? 5 ¿Cómo se llama su hermana?
1.4 (Personal preferences).
1.5 Thomas: un tinto, por favor. Alice: una coca-cola, por favor. Isabel: una taza de té con limón, por favor. Martín: Yo quiero una cerveza, por favor. You:
1.6 ¿Qué bocadillos hay?/Uno de jamón, por favor./¿Qué helados hay?/Uno de fresa, por favor.
1.7 1 (c). 2 (e). 3 (d). 4 (a). 5 (b).

2.1 1 (d). 2 (f). 3 (a). 4 (e). 5 (b). 6 (c).
2.2 1 Yo también hablo el inglés. 2 Yo también estudio idiomas. 3 Yo también trabajo en Londres. 4 Nosotros también hablamos el español. 5 Nosotros también estudiamos el español.
2.3 1 Se llama Eduardo. Es español de Madrid. Es contable. Tiene veinticuatro años. Es bajo y gordo. Tiene un hermano.
2.4 1 Yo vivo en Madrid. ¿Dónde vive usted? 2 Yo vivo en Tarragona, pero mi hermano vive en Valencia. 3 Nosotros vivimos en Toledo. Y vosotros, ¿dónde vivís? 4 Y ellos, ¿dónde viven? ¿En Salamanca? No, viven en Ciudad Real.
2.5 1 Son las cuatro. 2 Son las cuatro y cuarto. 3 Son las cuatro y veinte. 4 Son las cuatro y diez. 5 Son las cinco menos cuarto. 6 Son las cinco menos veinte. 7 Son las tres y media. 8 Son las cinco menos veinticinco.
2.6 1 Hay uno a las once veinticinco. 2 Hay uno a las quince treinta. 3 Hay uno a las cinco cuarenta y cinco. 4 Hay uno a las nueve treinta. 5 Hay uno a las diez treinta y cinco.
2.7 1 Son tres mil setecientas pesetas. 2 Son siete mil quinientas pesetas. 3 Son cuatro mil quinientas pesetas.
2.8 (a) ¿A qué hora sale el próximo tren para Sevilla?/¿A qué hora llega a Sevilla? (b) Uno, por favor./¿Qué línea es para Colón?/¿Tengo que hacer transbordo?

3.1 2 Sí, es verde. 3 No, es blanca. Es de algodón. 4 No, es azúl. Es de lana. 5 Sí, son grises.
3.2 Quisiera una camiseta./La cuarenta./Me gusta el estilo pero no me gusta el color./Me gusta más la azúl. ¿Puedo probármela?/Me parece bien. ¿Cuánto es, por favor?/Bueno, la compro.
3.3 1 No, es demasiado pequeño. ¿Hay otro más grande?/2 No, es demasiado larga. ¿Hay otra más corta?/3 No, es demasiado grande. ¿Hay otro más pequeño?/4 Son demasiado cortos. ¿Hay otros más largos?/5 Son demasiado pequeños. ¿Hay otros más grandes?
3.4 Belt: dos mil setecientas pesetas. Purse: nueve mil doscientas pesetas. Guitar: seis mil quinientas pesetas. Porrón: ochocientas pesetas. Necklace: doce mil seiscientas pesetas.
3.5 1 (c). 2 (f). 3 (d). 4 (b). 5 (a). 6 (e).
3.6 1 (e). 2 (h). 3 (d). 4 (g). 5 (b). 6 (c). 7 (f). 8 (a).
3.7 250 gramos de mantequilla; 1 litro de leche; 500 gramos de jamón de York; 1 paquete de galletas; 1 lata de sardinas; 1 kilo de plátanos; ½ kilo de melocotones, 6 peras maduras; 1 litro de aceite; 2 botellas de vino tinto; 12 huevos.
3.8 el café: ciento noventa ptas; 12 huevos: ciento noventa ptas; los plátanos: cien ptas; los tomates: trescientas ptas. Total: setecientas ochenta ptas.
3.9 Doscientos gramos de queso y cien gramos de jamón serrano, por favor./ medio kilo de manzanas y seis plátanos maduros./Un litro de leche, por favor. Eso es todo. ¿Cuánto es, por favor?
3.10 Buenos días, quisiera cambiar unos dólares, por favor./Ciento cincuenta dólares. ¿A cómo está el cambio hoy?/Deme dos billetes de cinco mil, tres billetes de mil y uno de quinientas pesetas.
3.11 Quiero dos de estos pasteles y una tarta, por favor./Sí, deme un donut y un panecillo./No, es para llevar.

EXERCISE KEY

4.1 Tome la primera calle a la izquierda. 2 Coja la segunda calle a la derecha. 3 Siga todo derecho. 4 Siga hasta el final de esta calle, y doble a la derecha.

4.2 1 La Catedral. 2 El Banco de España. 3 La Oficina de Turismo. 4 La Aduana. 5 La Plaza de Toros.

4.3 1 Lleno de super, por favor. 2 treinta y cinco litros de super, p.f. 3 ¿Quiere comprobar el aceite, p.f.? 4 ¿Quiere comprobar la presión, p.f.?

4.4 1 Mi coche no quiere arrancar. 2 El contacto no funciona. 3 ¿Puede mandar un mecánico, p.f.? 4 ¿Cuánto tiempo tardará?

4.5 Me duele el estómago y tengo diarrea./Desde hace una semana./ Muchas gracias, adiós.

4.6 ¿Puede darme algo para las picaduras de insecto?/Quiero un paquete de esparadrapos y unas pastillas para la garganta, p.f.

5.1 1 Quiero una habitación doble. 2 . . . sencilla. 3 . . . con ducha. 4 . . . con baño. 5 . . . con dos camas.

5.2 Buenas tardes, he reservado una habitación./Me llamo . . ./Está en el coche./Muchas gracias.

5.3 ¿Tiene una habitación?/No, sólo con lavabo./¿Cuánto es una habitación con baño?/Lo siento, es demasiado caro.

5.4 Buenas tardes. ¿Hay sitio, por favor?/Somos cuatro y tenemos una caravana./Una semana.

5.5 1 ¿Hay piscina? 2 ¿. . . duchas calientes? 3 ¿. . . .supermercado? 4 ¿. . . .restaurante? 5 ¿. . . .Correos?

5.6 1 No funcionan las duchas calientes. 2 No funcionan los retretes. 3 No funciona la electricidad. 4 No funciona el grifo. 5 No funciona el agua potable.

5.7 (choice of menus)

5.8 De primero, los mejillones./Pues, voy a tomar la sopa de pescado./De segundo, la merluza al horno./Entonces, ¿hay filete de lenguado?/Una naranja, por favor./Vale. Un plátano, por favor. La cuenta, por favor.

6.1 Me gusta el tenis y la natación./ No, no me gusta nada./Sí, pero prefiero el tenis.

6.2 Luisa: Me gusta el tenis, el baloncesto, el voleibol y el golf. Juan: Me gusta la natación, la vela, el windsurf y la pesca.

6.3 (a) Dos entradas, por favor./Son doscientas cincuenta pesetas./¿A qué hora están abiertas?/Se abren a las tres de la tarde. (b) Dos entradas, por favor./ Son ciento cincuenta pesetas./¿A qué hora se cierra?/Se cierra a las ocho.

6.4 1 (d). 2 (e). 3 (b). 4 (a). 5 (c).

6.5 2 ¿Conoce usted a Conchita, una amiga de mi esposa? 3 ¿Sabe jugar al ajedrez? 4 ¿Sabe usted cuándo se termina la reunión? 5 Sé que a mi esposa le gustaría mucho conocerle.

6.6 (personal preferences).

6.7 1 Art Exhibition. 2 Delgado is a painter; Teresa del Sol is a ceramist. 3 Open from Monday to Saturday. 4 From 6 pm to 8 pm. 5 10, Santa Catalina Street.

6.8 1 ¿Quedan localidades para la función de esta noche? 2 ¿Qué precio tienen las localidades? 3 ¿Quisiera dos entradas, por favor. 4 ¿Cuánto es, por favor? 5 ¿A qué hora empieza el espectáculo?

7.1 Me levanto a las siete y media./Me desayuno./Salgo a las nueve y voy en autobús a mi oficina./Sí, vuelvo a casa al mediodía para almorzar. Después, voy de compras y vuelvo a la oficina por la tarde.

7.2 Me levanté a las siete y media./Me desayuné./Salí a las nueve y fui en autobús a mi oficina./Volví a casa al mediodía para almorzar. Después fui de compras, y entonces volví a la oficina por la tarde.

7.3 Dígame./Me gustaría mucho. ¿A qué hora vendré? Sí, sé donde vives y cogeré un taxi.

7.4 Estudiaba el español./Vivía en la calle de Serrano con una familia española./Sí, había una hija./Se llamaba Mari-Carmen y tenía veintitrés años./ Salía con unos amigos, o me quedaba en casa y leía, o miraba la televisión./Sí, me gustaba mucho. Lo pasaba muy bien.

7.5 Fue . . . estaba . . . tenía . . . salió . . .

se dio . . . tenía . . . buscó . . . encontró
7.6 1 Cloudy. 2 Snow at high altitudes.
3 NW. 4 The coast. 5 −5°C.
7.7 1 Está despejado con olas de un
metro. 2 Hay tormentas. 3 Está muy
nuboso. 4 Hay nubes alternas. Hace
mucho calor. 5 Está muy nuboso con
lluvias y posibilidad de tormentas.

English–Spanish topic vocabularies

Numbers 0–100

0	cero						
1	uno/una	11	once	21	veintiuno	31	treinta y uno
2	dos	12	doce	22	veintidós	32	treinta y dos
3	tres	13	trece	23	veintitrés		etc.
4	cuatro	14	catorce	24	veinticuatro	40	cuarenta
5	cinco	15	quince	25	veinticinco	50	cincuenta
6	seis	16	dieciséis	26	veintiséis	60	sesenta
7	siete	17	diecisiete	27	veintisiete	70	setenta
8	ocho	18	dieciocho	28	veintiocho	80	ochenta
9	nueve	19	diecinueve	29	veintinueve	90	noventa
10	diez	20	veinte	30	treinta	100	cien, ciento

Numbers 101–1000

101	ciento uno	500	quinientos/as	first	primero/a
150	ciento cincuenta	600	seiscientos/as	second	segundo/a
200	doscientos/as	700	setecientos/as	third	tercero/a
250	doscientos cincuenta	800	ochocientos/as	fourth	cuarto/a
300	trescientos/as	900	novecientos/as	fifth	quinto/a
400	cuatrocientos/as	1000	mil	sixth	sexto/a
				seventh	séptimo/a

1,500 **mil quinientos/as** ground floor **planta baja** eighth octavo/a
2,000 **dos mil** 1st floor **primer piso** ninth noveno/a
20,000 **veinte mil** 3rd floor **tercer piso** tenth décimo/a
7,300 **siete mil trescientos**

The calendar and seasons The months (los meses del año)

		January	**enero**	July	**julio**
The seasons (las temporadas)		February	**febrero**	August	**agosto**
Spring	**la primavera**	March	**marzo**	September	**septiembre**
Summer	**el verano**	April	**abril**	October	**octubre**
Autumn	**el otoño**	May	**mayo**	November	**noviembre**
Winter	**el invierno**	June	**junio**	December	**diciembre**

Friday, February 2 **viernes, dos de febrero**
last week/next month **la semana pasada/el próximo mes**

VOCABULARY

Professions

accountant	contable	housewife	ama de casa
architect	arquitecto/a	journalist	periodista
businessman	hombre de negocios	lawyer	abogado/a
businesswoman	mujer de negocios	manager	director/a/gerente
civil servant	funcionario/a	nurse	enfermero/a
computer operator	operario/a de computadoras	plumber	fontanero/a
dentist	dentista	policeman	policía
designer	diseñador/ora	sales clerk	dependiente/a
doctor	médico/a	salesman	representante
employee	empleado/a	secretary	secretario/a
engineer	ingeniero/a	social worker	asistente social
farmer	agricultor/ora	teacher	profesor/ora
electrician	electricista	technician	técnico/a
		unemployed	desempleado/a

Clothes (la ropa) and accessories

. . . for women	. . . para mujeres
. . . for men	. . . para hombres
. . . for children	. . . para jóvenes
. . . for babies	. . . para niños
bag	el bolso
bathing suit	el traje de baño
belt	el cinturón
blouse	la blusa
bra	el sostén
briefs/pants	los calzoncillos
coat	el abrigo
dress	el vestido
gloves	los guantes
handkerchief	el pañuelo
hat	el sombrero
jacket	la chaqueta
jeans	los vaqueros
jumper (pullover)	el jersey
raincoat	el impermeable
scarf	la bufanda
(head)scarf	el pañuelo de cabeza
shirt	la camisa
shorts	los pantalones cortos
skirt	la falda
sleeves	las mangas
socks	los calcetines
stockings	las medias
suit	el traje
sweater	el suéter
tights	el panty
trousers	los pantalones
t-shirt	la camiseta

Shoes

boots	las botas
sandals	las sandalias
shoes	los zapatos
slippers	las zapatillas

Colors

color	el color
black	negro/a
blue	azul
brown	marrón
green	verde
grey	gris
red	rojo/a
white	blanco/a
yellow	amarillo/a
dark, light	oscuro/a, claro/a

Materials

acrylic	el acrílico
cotton	elalgodón
denim	el dril
leather	el cuero
nylon	el nilón
silk	la seda
suede	el ante
velvet	el terciopelo
wool	la lana

Note: You say: una falda **de** seda (= a skirt made of silk), and pantalones gris**es**, negr**os**, etc.; camisetas blanc**as**

VOCABULARY

Pharmaceutical items, etc.

aspirins	las aspirinas
bandage	la venda
band-aid	el esparadrapo
contraceptive pill	la píldora
cotton-wool	el algodón
insect repellent	el repelente para insectos
lozenges (throat)	las pastillas
pill, tablet	el comprimido
sleeping pill	el somnífero

Toiletries and other items

baby food	el alimento para bebé
comb	la peine
condoms	los condones
contraceptives	los anticonceptivos
diapers	los pañales
lipstick	el lápiz de labios
pacifier	el chupete
perfume	el perfume
razor blades	las hojas de afeitar
sanitary napkins	las compresas
shampoo	el champú
shaving cream	la crema de afeitar
soap	el jabón
sunglasses	las gafas de sol
suntan lotion	la crema bronceadora
tampons	los tampones
tissues	los pañuelos de papel
toilet paper	el papel higiénico
toothbrush	el cepillo de dientes
toothpaste	la pasta de dientes

Food shops

bakery	la panadería
butcher shop	la carnicería
pastry shop	la pastelería
confectionery	la confitería
dairy	la lechería
delicatessen	la mantequería
fish store	la pescadería
fruit shop	la frutería
grocery store	la tienda de alimentación, comestibles
market	el mercado
produce store	la verdulería
supermarket	el supermercado
wine merchant	la tienda de vinos, la bodega

Tobacco shop (el estanco)

cigar	el puro
cigarette	el cigarrillo
matches	los fósforos, las cerillas
newspaper	el periódico
magazine	la revista
postcard	la (tarjeta) postal
stamp	el sello
tobacco	el tabaco
(Virginian, black)	rubio, negro

Shops (las tiendas) and departments

bank	el banco
bookstore	la librería
camping equipment	el equipo de camping
clothes shop	la tienda de ropa
cosmetics, etc	la perfumería
dry cleaner's	la tintorería
hairdresser	la peluquería
hardware store	la ferretería
household (cleaning)	la droguería
newsstand	el quiosco
pharmacy	la farmacia
post office	el correos
shoe shop	la zapatería
stationery store	la papelería
tobacco shop	el estanco
toy store	la juguetería

Fish (el pescado), Shellfish (los mariscos)

anchovy	la anchoa
bass	la lubina
bream	el besugo
clams	las almejas
cod	el bacalao
crab	el cangrejo
hake	la merluza
lobster	la langosta
mussels	los mejillones
octopus	el pulpo
prawns	los langostinos
red mullet	el salmonete
salmon	el salmón
sardine	la sardina
shrimp	las gambas
skate	la raya
sole	el lenguado
squid	los calamares
trout	la trucha
tuna	el atún

VOCABULARY

Fruit (la fruta)

apple	la manzana
apricot	el albaricoque
banana	el plátano
cherry	la cereza
dates	los dátiles
grapes	las uvas
fig	el higo
lemon	el limón
melon	el melón
nuts	las avellanas
orange	la naranja
peach	el melocotón
pear	la pera
pineapple	la piña
plum	la ciruela
raspberry	la frambuesa
strawberry	la fresa
watermelon	la sandía

Vegetables (las verduras)

artichoke	la alcachofa
asparagus	los espárragos
beans (broad)	las habas
beans (French)	los frijoles
cabbage	la berza
carrots	las zanahorias
cauliflower	la coliflor
garlic	el ajo
lettuce	la lechuga
mushroom	el champiñón
olives	las aceitunas
onion	la cebolla
peas (chick)	los garbanzos
peas (green)	los guisantes
pepper (sweet)	el pimiento
potato	la patata
salad	la ensalada
tomato	el tomate

Meat (la carne), Poultry (las aves)

beef	la carne de res
chicken	el pollo
ham	el jamón
lamb	el cordero
pork	el cerdo
rabbit	el conejo
sausage	el salchichón
sausages	las salchichas
veal	la ternera

Bread, etc.

bread, loaf	el pan
bread roll	el panecillo
cake, pastry	el pastel
doughnut	el donut; el churro
tart, cake	la tarta, la torta

Groceries

biscuits, crackers	los bizcochos, las galletas
butter	la mantequilla
cheese	el queso
coffee	el café
eggs	los huevos
flour	la harina
margarine	la margarina
milk	la leche
oil	el aceite
pasta	la pasta
pepper	la pimienta
rice	el arroz
salt	la sal
sugar	el azúcar
tea	el té
vinegar	el vinagre

Parts of the car

battery	la batería
brake(s)	el freno, los frenos
carburetor	el carburador
clutch	el embrague
engine	el motor
exhaust	el tubo de escape
fanbelt	la correa de ventilador
headlight	el faro
ignition	el contacto
indicator	el intermitente
wheel	la rueda, el volante
windshield	el parabrisas
wipers	los limpiaparabrisas

Parts of the body

ankle	el tobillo
arm	el brazo
back	la espalda
blood	la sangre
bone	el hueso
chest	el pecho
ear	la oreja, el oído
elbow	el codo
eye	el ojo
face	la cara
finger	el dedo
foot	el pie
hair	el pelo, los cabellos

VOCABULARY

hand	la mano
head	la cabeza
heart	el corazón
knee	la rodilla
leg	la pierna
lung	el pulmón
mouth	la boca
muscle	el músculo
nose	la nariz
rib	la costilla
shoulder	el hombro
skin	la piel
stomach	el estómago
throat	la garganta
thumb	el pulgar
tooth	el diente
toe	el dedo del pie
wrist	la muñeca

Places to visit and natural features

bridge	el puente
building	el edificio
castle	el castillo, el alcázar
cathedral	la catedral
church	la iglesia
cloister	el claustro
house	la casa
monastery	el monasterio
mosque	la mezquita
museum	el museo
palace	el palacio
wall	el muro
cave	la cueva
hill	la colina
island	la isla
lake	el lago
mountain	la montaña
mountain range	la sierra
river	el río
sea	el mar
valley	el valle

Souvenirs (los recuerdos)

bull	el toro
castanets	las castañuelas
doll	la muñeca
fan	el abanico
necklace	el collar
pottery	la cerámica
pottery jug	el botijo

Sports and games

archery	el tiro con arco
athletics	el atletismo
basketball	el baloncesto
cards	las cartas
chess	el ajedrez
cycling	el ciclismo
fishing	la pesca
golf	el golf
horse riding	la equitación
judo	el yudo
jogging	el footing
rowing	el remo
sailing	la vela
shooting	la caza
soccer	el fútbol
swimming	la natación
tennis	el tenis
windsurfing	el windsurf
volleyball	el voleibol

Sports equipment

Where can I rent . . .	¿Dónde puedo alquilar . . .?
I'd like to rent . . .	Quiero alquilar . . .
a racket	una raqueta
some balls	unas pelotas
deck chair	una silla de lona
fishing rod	una caña
fishing net	una red
sunshade	una sombrilla
golf clubs	unos palos
ski boots	unas botas de ski
ski poles	unos bastones
skis	unos esquís
canoe	una canoa
dinghy	un bote, un barco
sailboat	un velero, un barco de vela
sail board	un windsurf
wetsuit	un traje de goma
championship	el campeonato
game	el juego
match, game	el partido
round of golf	una vuelta
stadium	el estadio
swimming pool	la piscina
tennis court	la pista de tenis
tournament	el torneo
track, course	la pista

VOCABULARY

Spanish-English Vocabulary

Note: the letters **ch, ll** and **ñ** are counted as individual letters in Spanish and words beginning with these combinations are listed after **c, l** and **n** respectively.

a to, at
abierto/a open
abridor *m.* bottle opener
abrir to open
abuelo, abuela grandfather, grandmother.
acabar to finish
accidente *m.* accident
aceite *m.* oil
aceituna *f.* olive
acrílico *m.* acrylic
acuerdo: de - agreed, I agree
adiós goodbye
aduana *f.* customs
aeopuerto *m.* airport
afición *f.* hobby
agencia *(f)* **de viajes** travel agency
agradable pleasant
agua water; **- potable** drinking water; **- mineral** mineral water
agujero *m.* hole
ahora now; **- mismo** this very moment
ajedrez *m.* chess
ajo *m.* garlic
albergue *(m)* **de juventud** youth hostel
albóndigas *f.pl.* meatballs
alcázar *m.* Moorish castle
alegre happy
alérgico allergic
algo something; **¿ - más?** anything else?
algodón *m.* cotton
algún, alguno some, any
almacén *m.* store; **los grandes almacenes** department store
almeja *f.* clam
almorzar to have lunch
almuerzo *m.* lunch
aquilar to rent
alquiler *(m)* **de coches** car rental
alto/a tall, high
amable kind, nice
ambulancia *f.* ambulance
amigo *m.* **amiga** *f.* friend
ancho/a wide
anchoa *f.* anchovy
andar to walk; **andando** walking
andén *m.* platform
anticiclón *m.* anticyclone
año *m.* year

aparatos eléctricos *m. pl.* electric appliances
aparcamiento *m.* parking space, parking lot
aparcar to park
apellido *m.* surname
aquí here
arrancar to start (a car)
arreglar to fix, mend
artículo *m.* article
asiento *m.* seat
autobús *m.* bus
autocar *m.* intercity bus
autopista *f.* freeway
avería *f.* breakdown
averiado broken (down)
avión *m.* airplane
ayer yesterday
ayudar to help
ayuntamiento *m.* town hall
azúcar *m.* sugar
azul blue

bailar to dance
bajar to go down, get down
bajo/a low, short; under
balcón *m.* balcony
banco *m.* bank
bañarse to bathe, take a bath
baño *m.* bathroom; bath
bar *m.* bar
barato/a cheap
barca *(f)* **de vela** sailboat
barco *m.* ship
barra *f.* bar, counter (inside bar)
bastante quite; enough
batido *m.* milkshake
beber to drink
bebida *f.* drink
biblioteca *f.* library
bien well
billete *m.* bill *(currency)*; ticket; **-de ida y vuelta** round-trip ticket
bistec *m.* steak
blanco/a white
boca *f.* mouth
bocadillo *m.* sandwich
bodega *f.* wine cellar
bolso *m.* handbag

VOCABULARY

bonito/a pretty
borrasca f. low-pressure area
botella f. bottle
buen, bueno/a good well; buenos días
  good morning; buenas tardes good
  afternoon
buscar to look for

cabeza f. head
cabina telefónica f. telephone booth
cada each
café m. coffee; - con leche coffee and
  milk; -solo black coffee
cafetería f. café
caja f. cashier; box
cala f. cove
calamar m. squid
caliente hot
calor m. heat; tengo - I am hot
calle f. street
cama f. bed; - matrimonial double bed
cámara f. camera
camarero m. waiter
cambiar to change
cambio m. change; currency exchange
camino m. way, road
camión m. truck
camisa f. shirt
camiseta f. t-shirt
camping m. campsite
caravana f. van
carne f. meat
carnet (m) de identidad identity card
carnicería f. butcher shop
caro/a expensive
carretera f. road, highway
carta f. menu; letter
cartelera f. entertainment page
casa f. house
casado/a married
castillo m. castle
catedral f. cathedral
caza f. shooting, hunting
ceda el paso give way; yield
cena f. dinner, supper
cenar to have dinner
centro m. center; - ciudad downtown
cepillo (m) de dientes toothbrush
cerca (de) near to
cercano near
cerdo m. pork
cerilla f. match
cerrado/a shut

cerrar to shut
cerveza f. beer
cheque (m) viajero traveler's check
cielo m. sky
cigarrillo m. cigarette
cine m. movie theater
cinturón (m) de seguridad seatbelt
circo m. circus
cita f. appointment
ciudad f. city
claro certainly, of course; light (adj)
cobro revertido m. collect call
cocina f. kitchen
coche m. car; coach (of train); - cama
  sleeping car; - litera berth
coger to take, catch
coja take (from coger)
colegio m. school
color m. color
collar m. necklace
comedor m. dining room
comer to eat
comida f. meal, lunch
como how, ask, like
¿cómo? how? what?
cómodo/a comfortable
completo/a full
comprar to buy
comprender to understand
compresa f. sanitary napkin
comprimido m. pill
computadora f. computer
con with
conejo m. rabbit
conocer to know (person or place)
consigna f. left luggage
controlar to check
coñac m. brandy
copa f. cup; tomar una - to have a drink
cordero m. lamb
correos post office
correspondencia f. connection (train)
corrida f. bullfight
corriente f. current (electric)
corto/a short
costa f. coast
costar to cost
crédito m. credit; tarjeta de - credit
  card; carta de - letter of credit
crema (f) de tomate tomato soup
cruce m. crossroads
cruzar to cross; cruzca cross over

VOCABULARY

¿cuál? which?

¿cuándo? when?

¿cuánto(s)?, ¿cuánta(s)? how much? how many?

cuarto m. room; - de dormir bedroom; - de estar living room; - de baño bathroom

cuarto m. quarter; - de hora quarter of an hour; - de kilo quarter of a kilo

cubierto m. cover charge; overcast (adj)

cubo (m) de basura trash bin

cuchara f. spoon; -da spoonful

cuchillo m. knife

cuenta f. bill; account; darse - de to realize

cuesta, cuestan it costs, they cost (from costar)

cueva f. cave

¡cuidado! careful!

champiñón m. mushroom

champú m. shampoo

chaqueta f. jacket

chica f. girl

chico m. boy

chocolate m. chocolate

choque m. collision

chorizo m. spicy sausage

chubasco m. shower (rain)

chuleta f. chop

dar to give; dame, deme give me

deber to owe

decir to say

dejar to leave

delante (de) in front (of)

delgado/a slim, thin

demasiado too, too much

deme give me (from dar)

dentista m/f. dentist

dentro (de) within

dependiente/a m/f. store clerk

deporte m. sport

derecha f. right; a la - on/to the right

derecho: todo - straight ahead

desayuno m. breakfast

descuento m. discount

desde since

desear to want

despacio: ir más - to slow down

despacho m. office; - de billetes ticket/office

despejado clear (sky)

después (de) afterwards, after

destino m. destination

desviación f. detour

detrás (de) behind

devuelve cambio gives change (from devolver to give back)

día m. day

diabético/a diabetic

diarrea f. diarrhea

diccionario m. dictionary

diente m. tooth; - de ajo clove of garlic

¡diga! ¡dígame! hello! (on telephone)

dinero m. money

dirección f. direction; - única one-way street; address

directo direct

disco m. record, disc

discoteca f. discotheque

divertirse to enjoy oneself

doblar to turn; doble a la derecha turn right

doble double

docena f. dozen

doctor m. doctor

doler to hurt, have a pain

domicilio m. residence

domingo Sunday

¿dónde? where?

dormir to sleep

ducha f. shower

duro m. 5-peseta coin

edificio m. building

el the (masc)

él, ella, he, she; him, her

electricidad f. electricity

ellos, ellas they; them

embarazada pregnant

empezar to begin

empresa f. company, firm

empujar to push

en in, on

encantar to delight

encender to light

encontrar to meet

enfermera f. nurse

enfermo/a ill

enfrente (de) opposite

ensaimada f. roll

ensalada f. salad

enseñar to show

entender to understand

entonces well, then

entrada *f.* entrance; entrance ticket; hors d'oeuvres
entregar to hand over; **entrega de equipajes** baggage check-in
enviar to send
equipaje *m.* luggage
equipo *m.* team
equitación *f.* horse-riding
es he, she, it is; you are (formal)
escalera *f.* staircase
escaparse to run away
escocés, escocesa Scottish
escuchar to listen
ese, esa that; **esos, esas** those; **eso** (neuter) that (pronoun)
eso that; **a eso de** about
español, española Spanish
esparadrapo *m.* band-aid
espárragos *m.pl.* asparagus
esposa *f.* wife
esquí *m.* ski; skiing; **- acuático** waterskiing
esta this; **estas** these (fem); **ésta** this (one); **éstas** these (ones)
estación *f.* station; **- de ferrocarril** railway station; **- de servicio** service station; **- de autobuses** bus station
estacionamiento *m.* parking
estadio *m.* stadium
estanco *m.* tobacco shop
estar to be
estatua *f.* statue
este this; **estos** these (masc); **éste** this (one); **éstos** these (ones)
estilo *m.* style
esto *(neuter)* this (pronoun)
estómago *m.* stomach
estrecho/a narrow, tight
estudiante *m/f.* student
estupendo/a great!
examen *m.* examination
excursión *f.* excursion
exposición *f.* exhibition
expreso *m.* express train
extranjero/a foreign; **al -** abroad

fábrica *f.* factory
falda *f.* skirt
farmacia *f.* pharmacy
fecha *f.* date
ferretería *f.* hardware store
ferrocarril *m.* railway

festivos: días - public holidays
ficha *f.* form
fideos *m.pl.* pasta (vermicelli, etc.)
fiebre *f.* fever; **- del heno** hay fever
fiesta *f.* festival, party
fila *f.* row
filete *m.* fillet
final: al - at the end
firma *f.* signature
firmar to sign
flan *m.* caramel custard
flauta *f.* flute
folleto *m.* brochure
formulario *m.* form
foto *f.* photograph
fresa *f.* strawberry
fresco/a cool
frío/a cool
frito/a fried
fruta *f.* fruit
frutería *f.* fruit store
fumar to smoke; **(no) fumador** (non) smoker
funcionar to work; **no funciona** it is not working
funcionario/a civil servant
fútbol *m.* soccer

gafas *f.pl.* glasses; **- de sol** sunglasses
galés, galesa Welsh
galleta *f.* biscuit, cracker; cookie
gamba *f.* prawn
ganas: tener - de to want to
garaje *m.* garage
gas: con - fizzy; **sin -** still (of drinks)
gaseosa *f.* fizzy drink
gasóleo *m.* diesel
gasolina *f.* gasoline
gasolinera *f.* gas station
gazpacho *m.* cold soup
gente *f.* people
gordo/a fat
gracias thank you
gramo *m.* gram
grande big; **los grandes almacenes** department stores
grave serious
grifo *m.* tap (faucet)
gripe *f.* influenza
gris grey
guapo/a handsome, pretty
guía *f.* guide-book; *m/f.* guide
guisantes *m.pl.* peas

VOCABULARY

guitarra *f.* guitar
gustar to like; **me gusta** I like

habitación *f.* room; - **doble** double room;
- **individual/sencilla** single room
hablar to speak
hacer to do; to make; **hace dos años**
two years ago; **hace sol** it is sunny;
hace frío/calor it is cold/hot
hacia towards
hambre *f.* hunger; **tengo** - I am hungry
hamburguesa *f.* hamburger
hasta until
hay there is, there are; - **que** one must
helado *m.* ice cream
herido/a hurt
hermano/a *m/f.* brother/sister
hielo *m.* ice
hígado *m.* liver
hijo/a *m/f.* son/daughter
hoguera *f.* bonfire
hola hello
hombre *m.* man
hora *f.* hour, time
horario *m.* timetable, schedule
hospital *m.* hospital
hostal *m.* family hotel
hotel *m.* hotel
hoy today
huevo *m.* egg

ida one-way (ticket) - **y vuelta** round trip
idioma *m.* language
iglesia *f.* church
importa: no - it doesn't matter
incluido/a included
información *f.* information
ingeniero *m.* engineer
inglés, inglesa English
insolación *f.* sunstroke
interesar to interest; -**se** to be
interested (in)
invierno *m.* winter
ir to go; -**se** to go away, leave
isla *f.* island
izquierda *f.* left; **a la** - on/to the left

jabón *m.* soap
jamón *m.* ham
jardín *m.* garden
jerez *m.* sherry
jersey *m.* pullover
juego *m.* game

jueves *m.* Thursday
jugar to play (game)
juguetería *f.* toy store

kilo *m.* kilogram
kilómetro *m.* kilometer

la, las the (feminine)
lado *m.* side; **al otro** - on the other side;
al - **de** beside
lana *f.* wool
largo/a long
lástima *f.* :¡Qué - ! What a pity!
lata *f.* tin; can
lavabo *m.* basin, washbasin
lavar to wash
leche *f.* milk
lechería *f.* dairy
leer to read
legumbres *f.pl.* vegetables, beans
lejos far; - **de** far from
lenguado *m.* sole
lentillas *f.pl.* contact lenses
lento slowly
levantarse to get up
libra *f.* pound
libre free, vacant
librería *f.* bookstore
libro *m.* book
limón *m.* lemon
limonada *f.* lemonade
línea *f.* line
liquidación *f.* clearance sale
lista *f.* list; - **de vinos** wine list
litro *m.* liter
localidad *f.* seat, ticket
lugar *m.* place
lunes *m.* Monday

llamar to call, telephone; -**se** to be
called
llave *f.* key
llegadas *f.pl.* arrivals
llegar to arrive
llenar to fill out; fill up
lleno/a full
llevar to buy, to take; to wear
llover to rain; **llueve** it is raining
lluvia *f.* rain

macarrones *m.* macaroni
madre *f.* mother
maduro/a ripe

VOCABULARY

mal, malo/a bad
maleta *f.* suitcase
manchego/a from La Mancha
mandar to send
mantequilla *f.* butter
manzana *f.* apple
mañana *f.* morning; tomorrow; **- por
    la** - tomorrow morning
mapa *m.* map
mar *m/f.* sea; **- arbolada** very rough sea
maravilloso/a wonderful
marca *f.* make (of car)
marcar to dial (a number)
mareado/a faint, dizzy
marido *m.* husband
mariscos *m.pl.* shellfish
martes *m.* Tuesday
más more
matrícula *f.* number (registration)
me me
mecánico *m.* mechanic
medias *f.pl.* stockings
médico *m.* doctor
medio/a half; **mediodía** noon; **media-
    noche** midnight; **y media** half past
mejillones *m.pl.* mussels
mejorarse to get better
melocotón *m.* peach
menos less
menú *m.* fixed price meal; menu
mercado *m.* market
merienda *f.* snack
merluza *f.* hake (codfish)
mermelada *f.* jam
mes *m.* month
mesa *f.* table
meter to put, insert
metro *m.* metro, subway; meter
mezquita *f.* mosque
mi, mis my
mí me (emphatic)
miércoles *m.* Wednesday
minuto *m.* minute
mirar to watch, look
mismo/a same
moderno/a modern
monasterio *m.* monastery
moneda *f.* coin, change
monumento *m.* monument
mostrar to show
mucho much; **muchísimo** very much
muebles *m.pl.* furniture
mujer *f.* woman

multa *f.* fine
museo *m.* museum
muy very

nacionalidad *f.* nationality
nada nothing; **de -** you're welcome;
    - más no more, that's all
nadar to swim
naranja *f.* orange
naranjada *f.* orangeade
nata *f.* cream
natación *f.* swimming
necesitar to need
negocios: de - on business
negro/a black
neumático *m.* tire
niebla *f.* fog
nieve *f.* snow
ningún, ninguno/a none, not any
niña *f.* little girl
niño *f.* child; little boy
no no, not
noche *f.* night
nombre *m.* name
normal regular (gas)
norte *m.* north
nosotros we, us
nube *f.* cloud
nublado, nuboso *m.* cloudy
nuevo/a new
número *m.* number; size (of shoe)

obra *f.* work; **obras** roadwork
ocupado occupied
oeste *m.* west
oficina *f.* office
ojo *m.* eye
olvidarse to forget
oscuro/a dark
otro/a other, another
oye listen (from **oír** to listen)

padre *m.* father; **-s** parents
pagar to pay
país *m.* country
palacio *m.* palace
pan *m.* bread
panadería *f.* bakery
panecillo *m.* bread roll
pantalones *m.pl.* trousers
papel *m.* paper; **-es de seguros**
    insurance papers

papelería *f.* stationery store
paquete *m.* packet, package
par *m.* pair
para to, for
parada *f.* bus stop
parar to stop
parecer to seem; **me parece que** I think that
parque *m.* park
partido *m.* match (soccer)
pasado/a previous, last; **la semana pasada** last week
pasaporte *m.* passport
pasar to spend (time); to pass; to happen
pasear to go for a walk
paseo *m.* walk; broad avenue
paso *m.* way
pasta *(f)* **de dientes** toothpaste
pastel *m.* pastry, cake
pastelería *f.* pastry shop
pastilla *f.* lozenge
patata *f.* potato
peaje *m.* toll
peatones *m.pl.* pedestrians
película *f.* film (in movies, etc.)
peligro *m.* danger
pelo *m.* hair
peluquería *f.* hairdresser
pensar to think
pensión *f.* boardinghouse; board; - **completa** full board; - **media** half board
pequeño/a small
pera *f.* pear
perdón pardon, excuse me
perfume *m.* perfume
perfumería *f.* cosmetics shop
periódico *m.* newspaper
periodista *m/f.* journalist
permiso *(m)* **de conducir** driver's license
persona *f.*person
pesca *f.* fishing
pescadería *f.* fish store
pescado *m.* fish
peseta *f.* peseta (unit of currency)
picadura *f.* sting
picar to sting
pie *m.* foot; **a** - on foot
pila *f.* battery
píldora *f.* contraceptive pill
pimienta *f.* pepper

pimiento *m.* pepper (green, etc.)
pinchazo *m.* flat (tire)
pintura *f.* painting
piscina *f.* swimming pool
piso *m.* floor (story); flat (apartment)
pista *f.* track, court; - **de tenis** tennis court
plano *m.* plan, map
planta *(f)* **baja** ground floor
plátano *m.* banana
plato *m.* plate, dish; - **combinado** meal on one plate
playa *f.* beach
plaza *f.* square; seat; - **de toros** bullring; **plazas libres** vacant seats
plomo *m.*lead
poco little, a little
poder to be able
policía *f.* police; *m.* police officer
pollo *m.* chicken
poner to put; to show (a film); **póngame** give me
por for, through, during, along; - **favor** please; - **aquí** this way; **¿por qué?** why?
porque because
porrón *m.* glass wine container
postal *f.* postcard
postre *m.* dessert
practicar to practice
precio *m.* price
preferir to prefer
prefijo *m.* area code (telephone)
preocuparse to worry
presentar to introduce
presión *f.* pressure
primavera *f.* spring
primer, primero/a first
primo *m.*, **prima** *f.* cousin
principios: a - de at the beginning (of)
probador *m.* fitting room
probarse to try on
profesor *m.*, **profesora** *f.* teacher
profundo/a deep
prohibido forbidden
pronóstico *m.* forecast
propina *f.* tip
próximo/a next
puede: ¿se puede? can one?
puente *m.* bridge
puerta *f.* door
puerto *m.* port
puesto *(m)* **de socorro** first-aid station

VOCABULARY

que what, that, than; ¿qué? what? which? how?; ¿qué tal? how are you? (informal)

quedar to keep, be left; quedarse to stay, remain

querer to want; quiero I want

queso *m.* cheese

¿quién? who?

quiosco *m.* newsstand

quisiera I would like

quizás perhaps

ración *f.* portion

rápido *m.* fast train

rato: un - a while

rebajas *f.pl.* bargains

recado *m.* message

recepción *f.* reception

receta *f.* prescription

recogida *(f)* de equipajes baggage claim

reducción *f.* reduction

refresco *m.* soft drink

reloj *m.* watch, clock

reparar to repair

reserva *f.* reservation

reservar to reserve

resfriado *m.* cold, flu

residencia *f.* guest house

respirar to breathe

restaurante *m.* restaurant

resto *m.* remainder

retraso *m.* delay

revista *f.* magazine

río *m.* river

robar to steal

roca *f.* rock

rodaja *f.* slice

rojo/a red

ropa *f.* clothes

rubio/a *m.* blonde

sábado Saturday

saber to know

sacacorchos *m.* corkscrew

sacar to take out, get (tickets)

saco *(m)* de dormir sleeping bag

sal *f.* salt

sala *(f)* de espera waiting room

salchichas *f.pl.* sausages

salchichón *m.* sausage

salida *f.* exit; salidas departures

salsa *(f)* de tomate tomato sauce

sándwich *(m)* caliente toasted sandwich

sangría *f.* red wine

secretaria *f.* secretary

seda *f.* silk

seguida: en - at once

seguir to follow, continue

segundo/a second; de - for the second course

seguro *m.* insurance; sure (adj)

sello *m.* stamp

semana *f.* week

sentar to fit, suit; -se to sit

sentirse to feel; lo siento I'm sorry

señor Mr., gentleman

señorita Miss, young lady

señora Mrs., lady

ser to be

serio serious

servicio *m.* service; -s toilets

sesión *(f)* continua continuous performance

si if

sí yes

siempre always

¡siga! follow! (from seguir)

simpático/a nice, pleasant

sin without

sitio *m.* place, site

sobre above, over; - todo especially

sol *m.* sun; hace - it is sunny

solo only; café - black coffee

soltero/a single (unmarried)

sombrero *m.* hat

somnífero *m.* sleeping pill

sopa *f.* soup

su his, her, its, their; your

subir to go up, climb

suéter *m.* sweater

super premium (gas)

supermercado *m.* supermarket

suplemento *m.* surcharge

sur *m.* south

tabla *(f)* a vela windsurfer

tacón *m.* heel

tal such; ¿qué tal? how are you?

talla *f.* size

taller mecánico *m.* workshop, garage

también also

tapas *f.pl.* appetizers

taquilla *f.* ticket window

tardar to delay, to take time

tarde *f.* afternoon, early evening; late

VOCABULARY

tarjeta *f.* card; - **postal** postcard; **tarjeta de crédito** credit card
tarta *f.* tart, cake
taxi *m.* taxi
taza *f.* cup
té *m.* tea
teatro *m.* theater
teléfono *m.* telephone
televisor *m.* television set
temperatura *f.* temperature
templado/a mild
temporal *m.* gale, storm
tenderse to lie down
tenedor *m.* fork
tener to have; **tengo hambre/sed** I am hungry/thirsty; **tengo veinte años** I am twenty years old
tenis *m.* tennis
terminar to finish; **terminado** finished
ternera *f.* veal
terraza *f.* terrace, balcony
tiempo *m.* weather
tienda *f.* store; - **de campaña** tent
tierra *f.* land
tinto *m.* red wine
tirita *f.* bandage
toalla *f.* towel; -**de baño** bathtowel
tocar to play (instrument)
todo all, every; everything; - **derecho** straight ahead
tomar to take; -**una copa** to have a drink
tomate *m.* tomato
tormenta *f.* thunderstorm
toro *m.* bull
tortilla *f.* omelette
tos *f.* cough
tostada *f.* toast
trabajar to work
trabajo *m.* work, job
traer to bring; **¡traiga!** bring!
traje *m.* suit; - **de baño** bathing suit
transbordo *m.* change, transfer
transeúnte *m.* passerby
tren *m.* train; -**es de cercanías** local trains; -**es de largo recorrido** long-distance trains
triste sad
trozo *m.* piece
tu your (informal)
tú you (informal)
turismo *m.* tourism
turista *m/f.* tourist

último/a last
un, uno/una a; one; unos/unas some
usted/ustedes you (formal)

vacaciones *f.pl.* vacation; **de** - on vacation
vainilla *f.* vanilla
¡vale! OK!
valer to cost, to be worth
valor *m.* value
valle *m.* valley
vamos let's go
vaqueros *m.pl.* jeans
vaso *m.* glass
vendedor *m.,* vendedora *f.* sales assistant
venir to come; **¡venga!** come here!
venta *f.* sale; -**anticipada** advance sales
ventana *f.* window
ver to see; **a** - let's see
verano *m.* summer
¿verdad? isn't it? aren't you? don't you?
verde green
verdulería *f.* produce store
verduras *f.pl.* vegetables
vermut *m.* vermouth
vestido *m.* dress
vez *f.* time; **una** - once; **dos veces** twice
vía *f.* track, platform
viajar to travel
viaje *m.* journey
viejo/a old
viento *m.* wind
viernes *m.* Friday
vinagre *m.* vinegar
vino *m.* wine
visitar to visit
vista *f.* view; - **del mar** sea view; **hasta la** - till we meet again
vivir to live
volver to return
vosotros you (plural)
vuelo *m.* flight
vuelta *f.* change; walk

y and
ya already
yo I

zapatería *f.* shoe store
zapatos *m.pl.* shoes
zumo *m.* juice